MANHATTAN PREP

Quantitative Comparisons & Data Interpretation

GRE® Strategy Guide

This volume focuses on two of the GRE's unique quantitative question types. The guide to Quantitative Comparisons briefs students on how to attack these problems and provides time-saving strategies. The guide to Data Interpretation demonstrates approaches to quickly synthesize graphical information on test day.

guide **6**

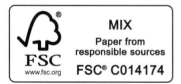

Quantitative Comparisons & Data Interpretation GRE Strategy Guide, Fourth Edition

10-digit International Standard Book Number: 1-937707-87-3
13-digit International Standard Book Number: 978-1-937707-87-3
eISBN: 978-1-941234-17-4

Layout Design: Dan McNaney and Cathy Huang
Cover Design: Dan McNaney and Frank Callaghan
Cover Photography: Amy Pierce

INSTRUCTIONAL GUIDE SERIES

SUPPLEMENTAL MATERIALS

MANHATTAN
PREP

June 3rd, 2014

Dear Student,

Thank you for picking up a copy of GRE *Quantitative Comparisons & Data Interpretation*. I hope this book provides just the guidance you need to get the most out of your GRE studies.

As with most accomplishments, there were many people involved in the creation of the book you are holding. First and foremost is Zeke Vanderhoek, the founder of Manhattan Prep. Zeke was a lone tutor in New York when he started the company in 2000. Now, 14 years later, the company has instructors and offices nationwide and contributes to the studies and successes of thousands of GRE, GMAT, LSAT, and SAT students each year.

Our Manhattan Prep Strategy Guides are based on the continuing experiences of our instructors and students. We are particularly indebted to our instructors Stacey Koprince, Dave Mahler, Liz Ghini Moliski, Emily Meredith Sledge, and Tommy Wallach for their hard work on this edition. Dan McNaney and Cathy Huang provided their design expertise to make the books as user-friendly as possible, and Liz Krisher made sure all the moving pieces came together at just the right time. Beyond providing additions and edits for this book, Chris Ryan and Noah Teitelbaum continue to be the driving force behind all of our curriculum efforts. Their leadership is invaluable. Finally, thank you to all of the Manhattan Prep students who have provided input and feedback over the years. This book wouldn't be half of what it is without your voice.

At Manhattan Prep, we continually aspire to provide the best instructors and resources possible. We hope that you will find our commitment manifest in this book. If you have any questions or comments, please email me at dgonzalez@manhattanprep.com. I'll look forward to reading your comments, and I'll be sure to pass them along to our curriculum team.

Thanks again, and best of luck preparing for the GRE!

Sincerely,

Dan

Dan Gonzalez
President
Manhattan Prep

HOW TO ACCESS YOUR ONLINE RESOURCES

If you…

⊳ **are a registered Manhattan Prep GRE® student**

and have received this book as part of your course materials, you have AUTOMATIC access to ALL of our online resources. This includes all practice exams, question banks, and online updates to this book. To access these resources, follow the instructions in the Welcome Guide provided to you at the start of your program. Do NOT follow the instructions below.

⊳ **purchased this book from the Manhattan Prep online store or at one of our centers**

1. Go to: www.manhattanprep.com/gre/studentcenter.

2. Log in using the username and password used when your account was set up.

⊳ **purchased this book at a retail location**

1. Create an account with Manhattan Prep at the website: www.manhattanprep.com/gre/createaccount.

2. Go to: www.manhattanprep.com/gre/access.

3. Follow the instructions on the screen.

Your online access begins on the day that you register your book at the above URL.

You only need to register your product ONCE at the above URL. To use your online resources any time AFTER you have completed the registration process, log in to the following URL: www.manhattanprep.com/gre/studentcenter.

Please note that online access is nontransferable. This means that only NEW and UNREGISTERED copies of the book will grant you online access. Previously used books will NOT provide any online resources.

⊳ **purchased an eBook version of this book**

1. Create an account with Manhattan Prep at the website: www.manhattanprep.com/gre/createaccount.

2. Email a copy of your purchase receipt to gre@manhattanprep.com to activate your resources. Please be sure to use the same email address to create an account that you used to purchase the eBook.

For any technical issues, email techsupport@manhattanprep.com or call 800-576-4628.

TABLE *of* CONTENTS

Chapter *of* 1

Quantitative Comparisons & Data Interpretation

Introduction

In This Chapter...

Chapter 1

Introduction

We know that you're looking to succeed on the GRE so that you can go to graduate school and do the things you want to do in life.

We also know that you may not have done math since high school, and that you may never have learned words like "adumbrate" or "sangfroid." We know that it's going to take hard work on your part to get a top GRE score, and that's why we've put together the only set of books that will take you from the basics all the way up to the material you need to master for a near-perfect score, or whatever your goal score may be. You've taken the first step. Now it's time to get to work!

How to Use These Materials

Manhattan Prep's GRE materials are comprehensive. But keep in mind that, depending on your score goal, it may not be necessary to get absolutely everything. Grad schools only see your overall Quantitative, Verbal, and Writing scores—they don't see exactly which strengths and weaknesses went into creating those scores.

You may be enrolled in one of our courses, in which case you already have a syllabus telling you in what order you should approach the books. But if you bought this book online or at a bookstore, feel free to approach the books—and even the chapters within the books—in whatever order works best for you. For the most part, the books, and the chapters within them, are independent; you don't have to master one section before moving on to the next. So if you're having a hard time with something in particular, you can make a note to come back to it later and move on to another section. Similarly, it may not be necessary to solve every single practice problem for every section. As you go through the material, continually assess whether you understand and can apply the principles in each individual section and chapter. The best way to do this is to solve the Check Your Skills and Practice Sets throughout. If you're confident you have a concept or method down, feel free to move on. If you struggle with something, make note of it for further review. Stay active in your learning and stay oriented toward the test—it's easy to read something and think you understand it, only to have trouble applying it in the 1–2 minutes you have to solve a problem.

Study Skills

As you're studying for the GRE, try to integrate your learning into your everyday life. For example, vocabulary is a big part of the GRE, as well as something you just can't "cram" for—you're going to want to do at least a little bit of vocab every day. So try to learn and internalize a little bit at a time, switching up topics often to help keep things interesting.

Keep in mind that, while many of your study materials are on paper (including Education Testing Service's [ETS's] most recent source of official GRE questions, *The Official Guide to the GRE revised General Test, Second Edition*), your exam will be administered on a computer. Because this is a computer-based test, you will *not* be able to underline portions of reading passages, write on diagrams of geometry figures, or otherwise physically mark up problems. So get used to this now. Solve the problems in these books on scratch paper. (Each of our books talks specifically about what to write down for different problem types.)

Again, as you study, stay focused on the test-day experience. As you progress, work on timed drills and sets of questions. Eventually, you should be taking full practice tests (available at www.manhattanprep.com/gre) under actual timed conditions.

The Revised GRE

As of August 1, 2011, the Quantitative and Verbal sections of the GRE underwent a number of changes. The actual body of knowledge being tested is more or less the same as it ever was, but the *way* that knowledge is tested changed. Here's a brief summary of the changes, followed by a more comprehensive assessment of the new exam.

The current test is a little longer than the old test, lengthened from about 3.5 hours to about 4 hours. When you sign up for the exam at www.ets.org/gre, you will be told to plan to be at the center for 5 hours, since there will be some paperwork to complete when you arrive, and occasionally test-takers are made to wait a bit before being allowed to begin.

Taking a four-hour exam can be quite exhausting, so it's important to practice not only out of these books, but also on full-length computer-based practice exams, such as the six such exams you have gained access to by purchasing this book (see page 7 for details).

There are now two scored Math sections and two scored Verbal sections. A new score scale of 130–170 is used in place of the old 200–800 scale. More on this later.

The Verbal section of the GRE changed dramatically. The Antonyms and Analogies disappeared. The Text Completion and Reading Comprehension remain, expanded and remixed in a few new ways. Vocabulary is still important, but is tested only in the context of complete sentences.

1

The Quant section of the new GRE still contains the same multiple-choice problems, Quantitative Comparisons, and Data Interpretations (which are really a subset of multiple-choice problems). The revised test also contains two new problem formats, which we will introduce in this section.

On both Verbal and Quant, some of the new question types have more than one correct answer, or otherwise break out of the mold of traditional multiple-choice exams. You might say that computer-based exams are finally taking advantage of the features of computers.

One way that this is true is that the new exam includes a small, on-screen, four-function calculator with a square root button. Many test-takers will rejoice at the advent of this calculator. It is true that the GRE calculator will reduce emphasis on computation—but look out for problems, such as percents questions with tricky wording, that are likely to foil those who rely on the calculator too much. *In short, the calculator may make your life a bit easier from time to time, but it's not a game changer.* There are **zero** questions that can be solved *entirely* with a calculator. You will still need to know the principles contained in the six Quant books (of the eight-book Manhattan Prep GRE series).

Finally, don't worry about whether the new GRE is harder or easier than the old GRE. You are being judged against other test-takers, all of whom are in the same boat. So if the new formats are harder, they are harder for other test-takers as well.

Additionally, graduate schools to which you will be applying have been provided with conversion charts so that applicants with old and new GRE scores can be compared fairly (GRE scores are valid for five years).

Exam Structure

The revised test has six sections. You will get a 10-minute break between the third and fourth sections and a 1-minute break between the others. The Analytical Writing section is always first. The other five sections can be seen in any order and will include:

- Two Verbal Reasoning sections (20 questions each in 30 minutes per section)
- Two Quantitative Reasoning sections (20 questions each in 35 minutes per section)
- Either an unscored section or a research section

An unscored section will look just like a third Verbal or Quantitative Reasoning section, and you will not be told which of them doesn't count. If you get a research section, it will be identified as such, and will be the last section you get.

1

Section #	Section Type	# Questions	Time	Scored?
1	Analytical Writing	2 essays	30 minutes each	Yes
2	Verbal #1	Approx. 20	30 minutes	Yes
3	Quantitative #1 *(order can vary)*	Approx. 20	35 minutes	Yes
10-Minute Break				
4	Verbal #2	Approx. 20	30 minutes	Yes
5	Quantitative #2 *(order can vary)*	Approx. 20	35 minutes	Yes
?	Unscored Section *(Verbal or Quant, order can vary)*	Approx. 20	30 or 35 minutes	No
Last	Research Section	Varies	Varies	No

All the question formats will be looked at in detail later in the chapter.

Using the Calculator

The addition of a small, four-function calculator with a square root button means that re-memorizing times tables or square roots is less important than it used to be. However, the calculator is not a cure-all; in many problems, the difficulty is in figuring out what numbers to put into the calculator in the first place. In some cases, using a calculator will actually be less helpful than doing the problem some other way. Take a look at an example:

> If x is the remainder when (11)(7) is divided by 4 and y is the remainder when (14)(6) is divided by 13, what is the value of $x + y$?

Solution: This problem is designed so that the calculator won't tell the whole story. Certainly, the calculator will tell you that $11 \times 7 = 77$. When you divide 77 by 4, however, the calculator yields an answer of 19.25. The remainder is not 0.25 (a remainder is always a whole number).

You might just go back to your pencil and paper, and find the largest multiple of 4 that is less than 77. Since 4 does go into 76, you can conclude that 4 would leave a remainder of 1 when dividing into 77.

1

(Notice that you don't even need to know how many times 4 goes into 76, just that it goes in. One way to mentally "jump" to 76 is to say, 4 goes into 40, so it goes into 80…that's a bit too big, so take away 4 to get 76.)

However, it is also possible to use the calculator to find a remainder. Divide 77 by 4 to get 19.25. Thus, 4 goes into 77 nineteen times, with a remainder left over. Now use your calculator to multiply 19 (JUST 19, not 19.25) by 4. You will get 76. The remainder is $77 - 76$, which is 1. Therefore, $x = 1$. You could also multiply the leftover 0.25 times 4 (the divisor) to find the remainder of 1.

Use the same technique to find y. Multiply 14 by 6 to get 84. Divide 84 by 13 to get 6.46. Ignore everything after the decimal, and just multiply 6 by 13 to get 78. The remainder is therefore $84 - 78$, which is 6. Therefore, $y = 6$.

Since you are looking for $x + y$, and $1 + 6 = 7$, the answer is 7.

You can see that blind faith in the calculator can be dangerous. Use it responsibly! And this leads us to…

Practice Using the Calculator!

On the revised GRE, the on-screen calculator will slow you down or lead to incorrect answers if you're not careful! If you plan to use it on test day (which you should), you'll want to practice first.

We have created an online practice calculator for you to use. To access this calculator, go to www.manhattanprep.com/gre and sign in to the student center using the instructions on the "How to Access Your Online Resources" page found at the front of this book.

In addition to the calculator, you will see instructions for how to use the calculator. Be sure to read these instructions and work through the associated exercises. Throughout our math books, you will see the ⊞ symbol. This symbol means "Use the calculator here!" As much as possible, have the online practice calculator up and running during your review of our math books. You'll have the chance to use the on-screen calculator when you take our practice exams as well.

Navigating the Questions in a Section

Another change for test-takers on the revised GRE is the ability to move freely around the questions in a section—you can go forward and backward one-by-one and can even jump directly to any question from the "review list." The review list provides a snapshot of which questions you have answered, which ones you have tagged for "mark and review," and which are incomplete, either because you didn't indicate enough answers or because you indicated too many (that is, if a number of choices is specified by the question). You should double-check the review list for completion if you finish the section early. Using the review list feature will take some practice as well, which is why we've built it into our online practice exams.

1

The majority of test-takers will be pressed for time. Thus, for some, it won't be feasible to go back to multiple problems at the end of the section. Generally, if you can't get a question the first time, you won't be able to get it the second time around either. With this in mind, here's the order in which we recommend using the new review list feature.

1. Do the questions in the order in which they appear.

2. When you encounter a difficult question, do your best to eliminate answer choices you know are wrong.

3. If you're not sure of an answer, take an educated guess from the choices remaining. Do NOT skip it and hope to return to it later.

4. Using the "mark" button at the top of the screen, mark up to three questions per section that you think you might be able to solve with more time. Mark a question only after you have taken an educated guess.

5. Always click on the review list at the end of a section, to quickly make sure you have neither skipped nor incompletely answered any questions.

6. If you have time, identify any questions that you marked for review and return to them. If you do not have any time remaining, you will have already taken good guesses at the tough ones.

What you want to avoid is surfing—clicking forward and backward through the questions searching for the easy ones. This will eat up valuable time. Of course, you'll want to move through the tough ones quickly if you can't get them, but try to avoid skipping around.

Again, all of this will take practice. Use our practice exams to fine-tune your approach.

Scoring

You need to know two things about the scoring of the revised GRE Verbal Reasoning and Quantitative Reasoning sections: (1) how individual questions influence the score, and (2) the score scale itself.

For both the Verbal Reasoning and Quantitative Reasoning sections, you will receive a scaled score, based on both how many questions you answered correctly and the difficulties of the specific questions you actually saw.

The old GRE was question-adaptive, meaning that your answer to each question (right or wrong) determined, at least somewhat, the questions that followed (harder or easier). Because you had to commit to an answer to let the algorithm do its thing, you weren't allowed to skip questions or to go back to change answers. On the revised GRE, the adapting occurs from section to section rather than from question to question (e.g., if you do well on the first Verbal section, you will get a harder second Verbal section). The only change test-takers will notice is one that most will welcome: you can now move freely about the questions in a section, coming back to tough questions later, changing answers after "Aha!" moments, and generally managing your time more flexibly.

1

The scores for the revised GRE Quantitative Reasoning and Verbal Reasoning are reported on a 130–170 scale in 1-point increments, whereas the old score reporting was on a 200–800 scale in 10-point increments. You will receive one 130–170 score for Verbal and a separate 130–170 score for Quant. If you are already putting your GRE math skills to work, you may notice that there are now 41 scores possible (170 − 130, then add 1 before you're done), whereas before there were 61 scores possible ([800 − 200]/10, then add 1 before you're done). In other words, a 10-point difference on the old score scale actually indicated a smaller performance differential than a 1-point difference on the new scale. However, the GRE folks argue that perception is reality: the difference between 520 and 530 on the old scale could simply seem greater than the difference between 151 and 152 on the new scale. If that's true, then this change will benefit test-takers, who won't be unfairly compared by schools for minor differences in performance. If not true, then the change is moot.

Question Formats in Detail

Essay Questions

The Analytical Writing section consists of two separately timed 30-minute tasks: Analyze an Issue and Analyze an Argument. As you can imagine, the 30-minute time limit implies that you aren't aiming to write an essay that would garner a Pulitzer Prize nomination, but rather to complete the tasks adequately and according to the directions. Each essay is scored separately, but your reported essay score is the average of the two, rounded up to the next half-point increment on a 0–6 scale.

Issue Task: This essay prompt will present a claim, generally one that is vague enough to be interpreted in various ways and discussed from numerous perspectives. Your job as a test-taker is to write a response discussing the extent to which you agree or disagree and support your position. Don't sit on the fence—pick a side!

For some examples of Issue Task prompts, visit the GRE website here:

www.ets.org/gre/revised_general/prepare/analytical_writing/issue/pool

Argument Task: This essay prompt will be an argument comprised of both a claim (or claims) and evidence. Your job is to dispassionately discuss the argument's structural flaws and merits (well, mostly the flaws). Don't agree or disagree with the argument—simply evaluate its logic.

For some examples of Argument Task prompts, visit the GRE website here:

www.ets.org/gre/revised_general/prepare/analytical_writing/argument/pool

Verbal: Reading Comprehension Questions

Standard five-choice multiple-choice Reading Comprehension questions continue to appear on the revised exam. You are likely familiar with how these work. Let's take a look at two *new* Reading Comprehension formats that will appear on the revised test.

Select One or More Answer Choices and Select-in-Passage

For the question type "Select One or More Answer Choices," you are given three statements about a passage and asked to "indicate all that apply." Either one, two, or all three can be correct (there is no "none of the above" option). There is no partial credit; you must indicate all of the correct choices and none of the incorrect choices.

> **Strategy Tip:** On "Select One or More Answer Choices," don't let your brain be tricked into telling you, "Well, if two of them have been right so far, the other one must be wrong," or any other arbitrary idea about how many of the choices *should* be correct. Make sure to consider each choice independently! You cannot use "process of elimination" in the same way as you do on normal multiple-choice questions.

For the question type "Select-in-Passage," you are given an assignment such as "Select the sentence in the passage that explains why the experiment's results were discovered to be invalid." Clicking anywhere on the sentence in the passage will highlight it. (As with any GRE question, you will have to click "Confirm" to submit your answer, so don't worry about accidentally selecting the wrong sentence due to a slip of the mouse.)

> **Strategy Tip:** On "Select-in-Passage," if the passage is short, consider numbering each sentence (i.e., writing 1 2 3 4 on your paper) and crossing off each choice as you determine that it isn't the answer. If the passage is long, you might write a number for each paragraph (I, II, III), and tick off each number as you determine that the correct sentence is not located in that paragraph.

Now give these new question types a try:

The sample questions below are based on this passage:

> Physicist Robert Oppenheimer, director of the fateful Manhattan Project, said, "It is a profound and necessary truth that the deep things in science are not found because they are useful; they are found because it was possible to find them." In a later address at MIT, Oppenheimer presented the thesis that scientists could be held only very nominally responsible for the consequences of their research and discovery. Oppenheimer asserted that ethics, philosophy, and politics have very little to do with the day-to-day work of the scientist, and that scientists could not rationally be expected to predict all the effects of their work. Yet, in a talk in 1945 to the Association of Los Alamos Scientists, Oppenheimer offered some reasons why the Manhattan Project scientists built the atomic bomb; the justifications included "fear that Nazi Germany would build it first" and "hope that it would shorten the war."

For question #1, consider each of the three choices separately and indicate all that apply.

1. The passage implies that Robert Oppenheimer would most likely have agreed with which of the following views:

    [A] Some scientists take military goals into account in their work
    [B] Deep things in science are not useful
    [C] The everyday work of a scientist is only minimally involved with ethics

2. Select the sentence in which the writer implies that Oppenheimer has not been consistent in his view that scientists have little consideration for the effects of their work.

(Here, you would highlight the appropriate sentence with your mouse. Note that there are only four options.)

Solutions

1. **(A)** and **(C):** Oppenheimer says in the last sentence that one of the reasons the bomb was built was scientists' *hope that it would shorten the war.* Thus, Oppenheimer would likely agree with the view that *Some scientists take military goals into account in their work.* (B) is a trap answer using familiar language from the passage. Oppenheimer says that scientific discoveries' possible usefulness is not why scientists make discoveries; he does not say that the discoveries aren't useful. Oppenheimer specifically says that ethics has *very little to do with the day-to-day work of the scientist*, which is a good match for *only minimally involved with ethics.*

Strategy Tip: On "Select One or More Answer Choices," write A B C on your paper and mark each choice with a check, an *X*, or a symbol such as ~ if you're not sure. This should keep you from crossing out all three choices and having to go back (at least one of the choices must be correct). For example, say that on a *different* question you had marked

A. *X*
B. ~
C. *X*

The answer choice you weren't sure about, (B), is likely to be correct, since there must be at least one correct answer.

---

2. The correct sentence is: **Yet, in a talk in 1945 to the Association of Los Alamos Scientists, Oppenheimer offered some reasons why the Manhattan Project scientists built the atomic bomb; the justifications included "fear that Nazi Germany would build it first" and "hope that it would shorten the war."** The word "yet" is a good clue that this sentence is about to express a view contrary to the views expressed in the rest of the passage.

1

Verbal: Text Completion Questions

Text Completions can consist of 1–5 sentences with 1–3 blanks. When Text Completions have two or three blanks, you will select words or short phrases for those blanks independently. There is no partial credit; you must make every selection correctly.

> Leaders are not always expected to (i) _____ the same rules as are those they lead; leaders are often looked up to for a surety and presumption that would be viewed as (ii) _____ in most others.

Blank (i)	Blank (ii)
decree	hubris
proscribe	avarice
conform to	anachronism

Select your two choices by actually clicking and highlighting the words you want.

Solution

In the first blank, you need a word similar to "follow." In the second blank, you need a word similar to "arrogance." The correct answers are *conform to* and *hubris*.

Strategy Tip: Do NOT look at the answer choices until you've decided for yourself, based on textual clues actually written in the sentence, what kind of word needs to go in each blank. Only then should you look at the choices and eliminate those that are not matches.

Now try an example with three blanks:

> For Kant, the fact of having a right and having the (i) _____ to enforce it via coercion cannot be separated, and he asserts that this marriage of rights and coercion is compatible with the freedom of everyone. This is not at all peculiar from the standpoint of modern political thought—what good is a right if its violation triggers no enforcement (be it punishment or (ii) _____)? The necessity of coercion is not at all in conflict with the freedom of everyone, because this coercion only comes into play when someone has (iii) _____ someone else.

Blank (i)	Blank (ii)	Blank (iii)
technique	amortization	questioned the hypothesis of
license	reward	violated the rights of
prohibition	restitution	granted civil liberties to

1

Solution

In the first sentence, use the clue "he asserts that this marriage of rights and coercion is compatible with the freedom of everyone" to help fill in the first blank. Kant believes that "coercion" is "married to" rights and is compatible with freedom for all. So you want something in the first blank like "right" or "power." Kant believes that rights are meaningless without enforcement. Only the choice *license* can work (while a *license* can be physical, like a driver's license, *license* can also mean "right").

The second blank is part of the phrase "punishment or _____," which you are told is the "enforcement" resulting from the violation of a right. So the blank should be something, other than punishment, that constitutes enforcement against someone who violates a right. (More simply, it should be something bad.) Only *restitution* works. Restitution is compensating the victim in some way (perhaps monetarily or by returning stolen goods).

In the final sentence, "coercion only comes into play when someone has _____ someone else." Throughout the text, "coercion" means enforcement against someone who has violated the rights of someone else. The meaning is the same here. The answer is *violated the rights of*.

The complete and correct answer is this combination:

Blank (i)	Blank (ii)	Blank (iii)
license	restitution	violated the rights of

In theory, there are 3 × 3 × 3, or 27 possible ways to answer a three-blank Text Completion—and only one of those 27 ways is correct. In theory, these are bad odds. In practice, you will often have certainty about some of the blanks, so your guessing odds are almost never this bad. Just follow the basic process: come up with your own filler for each blank, and match to the answer choices. If you're confused by this example, don't worry! The Manhattan Prep *Text Completion & Sentence Equivalence GRE Strategy Guide* covers all of this in detail.

Strategy Tip: Do not write your own story. The GRE cannot give you a blank without also giving you a clue, physically written down in the passage, telling you what kind of word or phrase must go in that blank. Find that clue. You should be able to give textual evidence for each answer choice you select.

Verbal: Sentence Equivalence Questions

For this question type, you are given one sentence with a single blank. There are six answer choices, and you are asked to pick two choices that fit the blank and are alike in meaning.

Of the Verbal question types, this one depends the most on vocabulary and also yields the most to strategy.

1

No partial credit is given on Sentence Equivalence; both correct answers must be selected and no incorrect answers may be selected. When you pick 2 of 6 choices, there are 15 possible combinations of choices, and only one is correct. However, this is not nearly as daunting as it sounds.

Think of it this way: if you have six choices, but the two correct ones must be similar in meaning, then you have, at most, three possible *pairs* of choices, maybe fewer, since not all choices are guaranteed to have a partner. If you can match up the pairs, you can seriously narrow down your options.

Here is a sample set of answer choices:

- [A] tractable
- [B] taciturn
- [C] arbitrary
- [D] tantamount
- [E] reticent
- [F] amenable

The question is deliberately omitted here in order to illustrate how much you can do with the choices alone, if you have studied vocabulary sufficiently.

Tractable and *amenable* are synonyms (tractable, amenable people will do whatever you want them to do). *Taciturn* and *reticent* are synonyms (both mean "not talkative").

Arbitrary (based on one's own will) and *tantamount* (equivalent) are not similar in meaning and therefore cannot be a pair. Therefore, the *only* possible correct answer pairs are (A) and (F), and (B) and (E). You have improved your chances from 1 in 15 to a 50/50 shot without even reading the question!

Of course, in approaching a Sentence Equivalence, you do want to analyze the sentence in the same way you would a Text Completion—read for a textual clue that tells you what type of word *must* go in the blank. Then look for a matching pair.

Strategy Tip: If you're sure that a word in the choices does *not* have a partner, cross it out! For instance, if (A) and (F) are partners and (B) and (E) are partners, and you're sure neither (C) nor (D) pair with any other answer, cross out (C) and (D) completely. They cannot be the answer together, nor can either one be part of the answer.

The sentence for the answer choice above could read as follows:

Though the dinner guests were quite _____ , the hostess did her best to keep the conversation active and engaging.

Thus, **(B)** and **(E)** are the best choices.

MANHATTAN
PREP

1

Try another example:

> While athletes usually expect to achieve their greatest feats in their teens or twenties, opera singers don't reach the _____ of their vocal powers until middle age.
>
> A   harmony
> B   zenith
> C   acme
> D   terminus
> E   nadir
> F   cessation

Solution

Those with strong vocabularies might go straight to the choices to make pairs. *Zenith* and *acme* are synonyms, meaning "high point, peak." *Terminus* and *cessation* are synonyms meaning "end." *Nadir* is a low point and *harmony* is present here as a trap answer reminding you of opera singers. Cross off (A) and (E), since they do not have partners. Then, go back to the sentence, knowing that your only options are a pair meaning "peak" and a pair meaning "end."

The correct answer choices are **(B)** and **(C)**.

Math: Quantitative Comparison

In addition to regular multiple-choice questions and Data Interpretation questions, Quantitative Comparisons have been on the exam for a long time.

Each question contains a "Quantity A" and a "Quantity B," and some also contain common information that applies to both quantities. The four answer choices are always worded exactly as shown in the following example:

$$x \geq 0$$

Quantity A	**Quantity B**
x	x^2

(A)   Quantity A is greater.

(B)   Quantity B is greater.

(C)   The two quantities are equal.

(D)   The relationship cannot be determined from the information given.

1

Solution

If $x = 0$, then the two quantities are equal. If $x = 2$, then Quantity (B) is greater. Thus, you don't have enough information.

The answer is **(D)**.

Next, take a look at the new math question formats.

Math: Select One or More Answer Choices

According to the *Official Guide to the GRE revised General Test*, the official directions for "Select One or More Answer Choices" read as follows:

> <u>Directions:</u> Select one or more answer choices according to the specific question directions.
>
> If the question does not specify how many answer choices to indicate, indicate all that apply.
>
> The correct answer may be just one of the choices or as many as all of the choices, depending on the question.
>
> No credit is given unless you indicate all of the correct choices and no others.
>
> If the question specifies how many answer choices to indicate, indicate exactly that number of choices.

Note that there is no partial credit. If three of six choices are correct, and you indicate two of the three, no credit is given. If you are told to indicate two choices and you indicate three, no credit is given. It will also be important to read the directions carefully.

Here's a sample question:

> If $ab = |a| \times |b|$ and $ab \neq 0$, which of the following must be true?
>
> Indicate <u>all</u> such statements.
>
>   [A] $a = b$
>   [B] $a > 0$ and $b > 0$
>   [C] $ab > 0$

Note that only one, only two, or all three of the choices may be correct. (Also note the word "must" in the question stem!)

1

Solution

If $ab = |a| \times |b|$, then you know ab is positive, since the right side of the equation must be positive. If ab is positive, however, that doesn't necessarily mean that a and b are each positive; it simply means that they have the same sign.

Answer choice (A) is not correct because it is not true that a must equal b; for instance, a could be 2 and b could be 3.

Answer choice (B) is not correct because it is not true that a and b must each be positive; for instance, a could be -3 and b could be -4.

Now look at choice (C). Since $|a| \times |b|$ must be positive, ab must be positive as well; that is, since two sides of an equation are, by definition, equal to one another, if one side of the equation is positive, the other side must be positive as well. Thus, answer **(C)** is correct.

Strategy Tip: Make sure to fully process the statement in the question (simplify it or list the possible scenarios) before considering the answer choices. That is, don't just look at $ab = |a| \times |b|$—rather, it's your job to draw inferences about the statement before plowing ahead. This will save you time in the long run!

Note that "indicate all that apply" didn't really make the problem harder. This is just a typical Inference-based Quant problem (for more problems like this one, see the Manhattan Prep *Number Properties* guide as well as the *Quantitative Comparisons & Data Interpretation* guide).

After all, not every real-life problem has exactly five possible solutions; why should problems on the GRE?

Math: Numeric Entry

This question type requires the test-taker to key a numeric answer into a box on the screen. You are not able to work backwards from answer choices, and in many cases, it will be difficult to make a guess. However, the principles being tested are the same as on the rest of the exam.

Here is a sample question:

If $x \Delta y = 2xy - (x - y)$, what is the value of $3 \Delta 4$?

1

<u>Solution</u>

You are given a function involving two variables, *x* and *y*, and asked to substitute 3 for *x* and 4 for *y*:

$$x \Delta y = 2xy - (x - y)$$
$$3 \Delta 4 = 2(3)(4) - (3 - 4)$$
$$3 \Delta 4 = 24 - (-1)$$
$$3 \Delta 4 = 25$$

The answer is **25**.

Thus, you would type 25 into the box.

Okay. You've now got a good start on understanding the structure and question formats of the new GRE. Now it's time to begin fine-tuning your skills.

MANHATTAN
PREP

Chapter 2

Quantitative Comparisons & Data Interpretation

The Basics

In This Chapter...

Chapter 2
The Basics

For Quantitative Comparison (QC) questions, you are to compare Quantity A with Quantity B and decide whether:

(A) Quantity A is greater.

(B) Quantity B is greater.

(C) The two quantities are equal.

(D) The relationship cannot be determined from the information given.

All of the first three answer choices have an implicit *always* before the word "greater" or "equal." The answer choices can really be thought of this way:

(A) Quantity A is *always* greater.

(B) Quantity B is *always* greater.

(C) The two quantities are *always* equal.

(D) The relationship cannot be determined from the information given or no consistent relationship exists.

An example problem can be used to demonstrate this principle:

Quantity A	**Quantity B**
$x(10 - x)$	25

If x is any number other than 5, Quantity B will be bigger than Quantity A. For instance, if x is 4, then Quantity A is $4(6) = 24$. If x is 7, Quantity A is $7(3) = 21$.

At this stage, that means that answers choices (A) and (C) are no longer possible. You know that Quantity A is not *always* bigger, and you know the values in the two quantities are not *always* equal.

A̸ B C̸ D

But that doesn't mean the answer is (B). When x is 5, Quantity A is 5(5) = 25. In that case, the values in the two quantities are equal. Although there are literally an infinite number of values of x that make Quantity B bigger, one counterexample is enough to make (B) the wrong answer. Quantity B is not *always* larger. Thus, the answer is **(D)**.

Trying to Prove (D)

This brings you to an important strategy that often comes into play when variables are involved. The secret is to always try to prove (D), to look for those numbers that will work differently than the first numbers you consider.

In the search for numbers that will produce different results, there are some types of numbers that tend to be more useful than others. They are positive numbers, negative numbers, fractions between 0 and 1, fractions between 0 and −1, and the numbers −1, 0, and 1.

Negative Numbers	Negative Fractions	Positive Fractions	Positive Numbers
$x < 0$	$-1 < x < 0$	$0 < x < 1$	$x > 0$

$$-1 \qquad 0 \qquad 1$$

It may seem like a lot of work to test all of these ranges for every Quantitative Comparison problem that involves variables, but there are a few things that can save you some time without preventing you from doing a thorough job.

The first thing that helps is that, as mentioned above, one counterexample is enough to make (D) the correct answer. As you get better at identifying which ranges of numbers will produce different results, you will need to test fewer options.

The second thing that helps is that some problems provide constraints on the variables involved in the question. This helps by eliminating some possible ranges. Take this problem, for example:

y is an integer.

Quantity A	**Quantity B**
$\dfrac{1}{2^y}$	$\dfrac{1}{3^y}$

2

Because y is an integer, you know that you do not need to try positive and negative fractions. At the same time, you should try to pick numbers that are easy to work with and will have a high potential impact. Begin with the number 1. If y equals 1, then Quantity A will be 1/2 and Quantity B will be 1/3. That means that Quantity A is bigger, and that (B) and (C) are no longer possible answer choices.   A ̶B̶ ̶C̶ D

Another easy number is 0. If $y = 0$, then Quantity A is 1, because $2^0 = 1$. Similarly, Quantity B is 1, because 3^0 also equals 1. So the values of the two quantities are equal. Therefore, (A) is no longer possible. You've found one case for which Quantity A is larger, and one for which the two quantities are equal. Thus, the correct answer is **(D)**.

Zero was a good number to try for a couple of reasons. First, as mentioned, the calculations were easy to perform. Second, because the variable was an exponent, you were able to make use of the rule that any number when raised to a power of 0 equals 1. Even though you had two different bases, you managed to make them, and the quantities, equal.

Strategy Tip: When you **try to prove (D)**, plug in numbers from different parts of the number line (e.g., −1, 0, 1)

Compare, Don't Calculate

For a variety of reasons, Educational Testing Service (ETS) wants to ask questions on the Quantitative section of the GRE that quickly test your ability to reason about quantities, but that don't rely too much on raw computational ability. The QC questions were developed specifically to fill this role. On many questions, you will be tempted to use the on-screen calculator, but using the calculator will often be more trouble than it's worth.

For the most part, the best way to approach QC questions is to take advantage of the opportunities to avoid computation that the test makers deliberately give you, and to avoid the traps that they deliberately set. Though some test-prep purveyors like to talk about "beating the test" or "cracking the code," the truth is that ETS, the people who invented this format, and who write the GRE and SAT among many other tests, deliberately create opportunities for the savvy test-taker. This example problem demonstrates the principle nicely:

Quantity A	**Quantity B**
$\dfrac{1}{\frac{1}{2}+\frac{1}{4}+\frac{1}{8}}$	$\dfrac{1}{2}+\dfrac{1}{4}+\dfrac{1}{8}$

2

On the surface, this problem seems to involve a lot of fractions that must be added together, which can be time consuming. On top of that, there is a complex fraction in Quantity A that could further slow you down. But there is no need for this level of computation. Notice that Quantity B, $\frac{1}{2}+\frac{1}{4}+\frac{1}{8}$, is less than $\frac{1}{2}+\left(\frac{1}{4}+\frac{1}{4}\right)$, and so must be less than 1. This means that the numerator in Quantity A (1) is greater than the denominator $\frac{1}{2}+\frac{1}{4}+\frac{1}{8}$, and so the entire fraction is greater than 1. You don't have to actually add the fractions in the expression $\frac{1}{2}+\frac{1}{4}+\frac{1}{8}$. The correct answer is **(A)**. (The fractions add up to $\frac{7}{8}$, by the way.)

In this problem, you can determine the correct answer solely by making the distinction that Quantity B is less than 1, while Quantity A is greater than 1. Much of your preparation for QCs will revolve around your ability to identify these quick distinctions that can save you time and energy spent performing unnecessary calculations. Try another example:

Quantity A	**Quantity B**
$\frac{1}{4}-\frac{1}{5}+\frac{1}{6}-\frac{1}{7}+\frac{1}{8}$	$\frac{1}{4}$

If you're tempted to actually evaluate the expression on the left with the calculator—STOP! It will take a lot of time and energy. In this case, all you need to do is compare the two values. The first fraction in the expression in Quantity A is $\frac{1}{4}$, which is the same as the fraction in Quantity B. All you have to do is determine whether the remaining fractions will increase or decrease your starting value, which is a lot less work.

You can group the remaining fractions into groups of two. What is the net effect of subtracting $\frac{1}{5}$ and adding $\frac{1}{6}$? $\frac{1}{5}$ is greater than $\frac{1}{6}$, so the net effect is negative. Similarly, subtracting $\frac{1}{7}$ and adding $\frac{1}{8}$ will also make the value smaller. Without knowing the exact value of the expression on the left, you can be sure that it will be smaller than the value on the right. The correct answer is **(B)**.

As you practice answering QC questions, you should always be on the lookout for ways to reduce the amount of computation required to arrive at an answer. To close out this section, here are some strategies that can be employed to reduce your workload on some QC questions.

The Invisible Inequality

Some QC problems are difficult simply because one or both of the quantities are written in such a way that makes direct comparisons difficult. Take this problem, for example:

$$x > 0$$

Quantity A	**Quantity B**
$\dfrac{4x^2+2x^2+3x+9}{2x}$	$2x+x+\dfrac{3}{2}+\dfrac{18}{4x}$

2

You could try plugging in a number for x, but it would be time consuming, even if you pick a simple number like 1. Additionally, how would plugging in a single number for x convince you that the conclusion was always valid? You would still need to try to prove (D), taking yet more time.

Fortunately, there's a better way. All QC questions can be thought of as giant inequalities. To that end, there are a few things you're allowed to do to both sides. You can:

1. Add or subtract the same value to both quantities.
2. Multiply or divide both quantities by the same number, as long as it is positive.
3. Square or square root both quantities if you're sure they are both positive.

In this case, you're given a piece of common information telling you that $x > 0$. This is a signal telling you that you're allowed to multiply or divide both sides by x. On further thought, you'd probably be better off multiplying both quantities by $2x$, because it will get rid of the denominator in Quantity A. Treat the two quantities as if they are on opposite sides of an inequality. Because you don't know which direction the inequality faces, use a (?) as a place holder.

$$2x\left(\frac{4x^2 + 2x^2 + 3x + 9}{2x}\right) \qquad ? \qquad 2x\left(2x + x + \frac{3}{2} + \frac{18}{4x}\right)$$

$$\cancel{2x}\left(\frac{4x^2 + 2x^2 + 3x + 9}{\cancel{2x}}\right) \qquad ? \qquad 2x(2x) + 2x(x) + \cancel{2}x\left(\frac{3}{\cancel{2}}\right) + \cancel{2}\cancel{x}\left(\frac{18}{\cancel{4}_2\,\cancel{x}}\right)$$

$$4x^2 + 2x^2 + 3x + 9 \qquad ? \qquad 4x^2 + 2x^2 + 3x + 9$$

The two quantities are equal! You can save a whole lot of time by not plugging in numbers, so always keep the **invisible inequality** in mind. The answer is **(C)**.

Quantity B as Benchmark

Using Quantity B as a benchmark can often provide you some insight into the problem at hand and save you some time. Take this problem, for example:

A discount of 30% off the original selling
price of a dress reduced the price to $99.

Quantity A	Quantity B
The original selling price	$150

There are two approaches to this problem. Both will get you there, but you want the method that will get you there more quickly. Instead of setting up an equation to solve for the original price of the sweater, assume the original price was $150, Quantity B.

2

If the original price was $150, and it was reduced 30%, you can use the calculator to calculate the discounted price very quickly: 30% of 150 is 0.3 × 150 = $45. That means the discounted price is $150 − $45 = $105.

An original price of $150 with a 30% discount would have made the new price $105, which is higher than the discount price stipulated in the additional information. Therefore, the original price of the sweater must have been less than $150. The answer is **(B)**.

If Quantity B is a number and Quantity A requires calculation of some kind, see if you can simplify equations and reduce the amount of necessary computation by using Quantity B as a benchmark.

Quantity B can also help in a slightly different, but related, way. Earlier in this chapter was a discussion about trying to prove (D). Sometimes the best way to prove (D) is by trying to prove (C) using Quantity B as a guide.

Quantity A	**Quantity B**
The perimeter of Triangle *ABC*, an isosceles triangle whose longest side is equal to 11	22

Though there is no picture given, it should be easy to imagine a triangle that has a perimeter greater than 22. If one of the other sides also has a length of 11, then no matter the length of the third side, the perimeter will be greater than 22. So now your goal is to find a triangle that has a perimeter of 22 or less. The number 22 provides you with a goal, so that you do not have to search blindly and create random isosceles triangles that get you no closer to an answer.

If one of the sides is 11, that means that the remaining two sides must have a combined length of 11 if you are to achieve your goal. You have already seen what happens if the two equal sides each have a length of 11. Therefore, for the triangle to remain isosceles, the two unknown sides must be equal. The only way they could be equal is if they each have a length of 5.5.

Careful! There is a trap here. Remember, any two sides of a triangle must add up to **greater than** the length of the other side or else you can't actually connect all three sides. So this triangle cannot, in fact, exist. Similarly, the two sides cannot be less than 5.5, so you know that the perimeter of Triangle *ABC* will be greater than 22. The answer is **(A)**.

By specifically trying to make the two values equal, you were able to prove that Quantity A will always be greater. Trying to prove (C) saved you time by giving you a specific value to focus on.

If you are unsure of the geometry rules that were used to solve this question, don't worry. You'll get a proper review in the *Geometry GRE Strategy Guide*.

It is worth saying again that the strategies laid out are only some of the shortcuts available to a test-taker with a trained eye. In general, your motto should be: Less is More. Good test-takers are always vigilant, always looking for ways to reduce their computational burden.

The next section of this book explores areas of interest organized by content area: Algebra, Fractions, Decimals, & Percents, Geometry, Number Properties, and Word Problems. Remember, this is still a math test, and a good understanding of fundamental rules and formulas is still essential to a good score.

2

Strategy Tips: Some of the strategies you will be employing on Quantitative Comparisons are:

Try to Prove (D).

Use −1, 0, and 1.

Use positive numbers greater than 1 and fractions between 0 and 1.

Use negative numbers less than −1 and fractions between 0 and −1.

Use the Invisible Inequality.

Add or subtract to both quantities.

Multiply or divide both quantities by a positive number.

Square or square root both quantities if they are positive.

Use Quantity B as a Benchmark.

Use when Quantity B is a number (no variables).

When Quantity A requires calculation, try to save time by using Quantity B.

Use Quantity B as a guide to try to prove (C).

Chapter 3

Quantitative Comparisons & Data Interpretation

Algebra

In This Chapter...

Chapter 3
Algebra

Finding quick solutions is a fairly general theme on Quantitative Comparisons, but nowhere is this theme more relevant than with algebra. If you generally associate algebra with long complicated equations, isolating variables, solving systems of equations with two or even three variables, etc., you're in for a treat. Bottom line: you will not have to do a lot of algebra on QC questions. This is not to say that Algebra questions are easier than questions in other content areas, but many equations that appear on QC can be simplified in just a few steps. This chapter discusses how the GRE tests your understanding of algebraic principles on QC. Note that this chapter will assume basic familiarity with algebraic concepts and will only focus on principles of QC questions. For more specifics on algebraic concepts, see the *Manhattan Prep Algebra GRE Strategy Guide*.

Equations

The most important thing you have to figure out on QC Algebra questions is when you are allowed to plug in a number, and when you are not. In other words, when is a variable not a variable?

Consider this example. Can you plug in numbers?

$$x - 3 = 12$$
$$y + 2x = 40$$

Quantity A	**Quantity B**
y	9

Pay attention to any constraints that have been placed on variables. In this question, the first equation gives you enough information to find the value of x. And because you have enough information to find x, you also have enough information to find y through the second equation. In fact, $x = 15$, which means that y will equal 10, and thus the answer to this question is **(A)**. Although y is a variable, it actually has a definite value.

Problem Recap: When variables have a **unique value**, you must solve for the value of the variable.

On this test, variables can assume a variety of forms. They can:

1. Have one unique value (as in the problem above)
2. Have a range of possible values (i.e., $-3 < z < 2$)
3. Have no constraints.
4. Be defined in terms of other variables.

On any question that involves variables, you should identify which situation you are dealing with. Take this problem, for example:

$$2 \leq z \leq 4$$

Quantity A	**Quantity B**
$\dfrac{2z}{5}$	$\dfrac{5}{2z}$

In this problem, z doesn't have one specific value, but its range is well-defined. In a situation such as this, you should examine the upper and lower bounds of z.

Start with the lower bound. Plug in 2 for z in both quantities:

$$2 \leq z \leq 4$$

Quantity A	**Quantity B**
$\dfrac{2(2)}{5} = \dfrac{4}{5}$	$\dfrac{5}{2(2)} = \dfrac{5}{4}$

When $z = 2$, Quantity B is bigger.   A̶ B C̶ D

Now try the upper bound. Plug in 4 for z in both quantities:

$$2 \leq z \leq 4$$

Quantity A	**Quantity B**
$\dfrac{2(4)}{5} = \dfrac{8}{5}$	$\dfrac{5}{2(4)} = \dfrac{5}{8}$

When $z = 4$, Quantity A is bigger. The correct answer is **(D)**.

The way in which variables are constrained (or not) can tell you a lot about efficient ways to approach that particular problem.

Strategy Tip: If a variable has a **defined range**, you need to test the **boundaries** of that range.

MANHATTAN
PREP

Relationship Only

Another way variables can be defined on this test is in terms of another variable. Take the following example:

$$\frac{x+5}{5} = \frac{y+6}{6}$$

Quantity A	**Quantity B**
6x	5y

In this problem, you are given an equation that contains two variables: x and y. You won't be able to solve for the value of either variable, but that doesn't mean the answer will be (D). For this type of problem, the best course of action is to make a *direct comparison* of the variables. You can do this by *simplifying* the equation so that all unnecessary terms have been eliminated. Begin by cross-multiplying:

$6(x + 5) = 5(y + 6)$
$6x + 30 = 5y + 30$

Now you have a 30 on each side that should be eliminated:

$6x = 5y$

You still don't know the value of either variable, but you do have enough information to answer the question. The answer is **(C)**.

Problem Recap: If a variable is defined in terms of another variable, **simplify** and find a **direct comparison**.

No Constraints

Sometimes, you will not be given any information about a variable. If there are no constraints on the variable, then your goal is to prove (D). For example:

Quantity A	**Quantity B**
$\dfrac{x}{2}$	2x

No information about x has been given. If x is positive, Quantity B will be bigger. For instance, if $x = 1$,

Quantity A = $\dfrac{1}{2}$ and Quantity B = 2.   A̸ B C̸ D

However, there is no reason x must be positive. Remember, one way to try to prove (D) is to check negative possibilities. If x is negative, then Quantity A will be bigger. For instance, if $x = -1$, then Quantity

$A = -\dfrac{1}{2}$ and Quantity B $= -2$.

~~A~~ ~~B~~ ~~C~~ D

The correct answer is (D).

Strategy Tip: If a variable has no constraints, **try to prove (D)**.

---

3 Certain Properties

Finally, variables may be defined as having certain properties. The most common include a variable being positive or negative or an integer. The strategy for this type of problem is identical to the strategy for problems in which variables have no constraints: prove (D). The only difference is that the types of numbers you can use are restricted. This type is also similar to Range of Values, in that you should test extreme values of the possible range.

x is positive.

Quantity A	**Quantity B**
$x(x + 1)$	$x(x^2 + 1)$

Begin by distributing both quantities:

x is positive.

Quantity A	**Quantity B**
$x(x + 1) = x^2 + x$	$x(x^2 + 1) = x^3 + x$

Both sides have an x, which you can cancel out.

x is positive.

Quantity A	**Quantity B**
$\begin{array}{r} x^2 + x \\ -\ x \\ \hline x^2 \end{array}$	$\begin{array}{r} x^3 + x \\ -\ x \\ \hline x^3 \end{array}$

You know x is positive, so x can't be negative or 0. If $x = 2$, then Quantity A = 4 and Quantity B = 8.

~~A~~ B ~~C~~ D

In order to be thorough, however, make sure that you try numbers that have a chance of behaving differently. You can't try negatives, but you can try 1 and fractions between 0 and 1. If $x = 1$, then Quantity A = 1 and Quantity B = 1. Also, if x were a positive fraction (e.g., 1/2), then Quantity A would be greater than Quantity B. The correct answer is **(D)**.

Strategy Tips: Variables are used in many ways on this test. How they're presented can often give you a clue as to the appropriate strategy to employ. To recap:

If a variable:	then:
has a unique value (e.g., $x + 3 = -5$)	solve for the value of the variable
has a defined range (e.g., $-4 \leq w \leq 3$)	test the boundaries
has a relationship with another variable (e.g., $2p = r$)	simplify the equation and make a direct comparison of the variables
has no constraints	try to prove (D)
has specific properties (e.g., x is negative)	try to prove (D)

3

Quadratic Equations

The issue of quadratic equations can be boiled down to one principle: know how to FOIL well. Many questions concerning quadratic equations hinge on your ability to FOIL factored expressions correctly.

The quadratic equation can appear either in one or both of the quantities *or* in the common information. Where it is will determine how you approach the question.

Quadratics in Quantities

If the quadratic equation appears in the quantities, then your goal is to FOIL and eliminate common terms to make a direct comparison.

$$pq \neq 0$$

Quantity A	**Quantity B**
$(2p + q)(p + 2q)$	$p^2 + 5pq + q^2$

In order to make a meaningful comparison between the two quantities, you have no choice but to FOIL Quantity A.

You get:

First $= 2p \cdot p = 2p^2$
Outside $= 2p \cdot 2q = 4pq$
Inside $= q \cdot p = pq$
Last $= q \cdot 2q = 2q^2$

The expression on the left equals $2p^2 + 5pq + 2q^2$. Both quantities contain the term $5pq$, which you can safely subtract. The comparison becomes:

$$pq \neq 0$$

Quantity A   **Quantity B**

$$\begin{array}{r} 2p^2 + 5pq + 2q^2 \\ -5pq \\ \hline \mathbf{2p^2} \quad +\mathbf{2q^2} \end{array}$$ $$\begin{array}{r} p^2 + 5pq + q^2 \\ -5pq \\ \hline p^2 \quad +q^2 \end{array}$$

The information at the top tells you that neither p nor q can be 0, and you know that p^2 and q^2 will both be positive, so you can now definitely say that Quantity A is larger than Quantity B. To answer this question correctly, you had to do two things: 1) FOIL Quantity A (the faster the better), and 2) eliminate common terms from both quantities and compare the remaining terms. The correct answer is **(A)**.

Strategy Tip: When a quadratic appears in one or both quantities, FOIL the quadratics, eliminate common terms, and compare the quantities.

As QC questions involving quadratic equations get more difficult, they can make either FOILing or simplifying more difficult. Try this example problem:

$$r > s$$

Quantity A   **Quantity B**

$(r + s)(r - s)$ $(s + r)(s - r)$

This problem now requires you to FOIL two expressions, not just one (you can't simply divide out $(r + s)$ from each side, because $(r + s)$ might be negative). However, this is where knowledge of special products can save you some time. Each of these expressions is a difference of squares:

$$r > s$$

Quantity A   **Quantity B**

$(r + s)(r - s) = \mathbf{r^2 - s^2}$ $(s + r)(s - r) = \mathbf{s^2 - r^2}$

Now you need to be able to compare these expressions. You know r is greater than s, so it might be tempting to conclude that Quantity A is greater than Quantity B. Plug in $r = 3$ and $s = 2$:

$$r > s$$

Quantity A   **Quantity B**

$r^2 - s^2 =$ $s^2 - r^2 =$

$9 - 4 = \mathbf{5}$ $4 - 9 = \mathbf{-5}$

Quantity A is greater than Quantity B.   A ~~B~~ ~~C~~ D

But there's a problem. You know r is greater than s, but you don't know the sign of either variable. Remember to check negative possibilities!

Now plug in $r = -2$ and $s = -3$:

$$r > s$$

Quantity A	**Quantity B**
$r^2 - s^2 =$	$s^2 - r^2 =$
$4 - 9 = \mathbf{-5}$	$9 - 4 = \mathbf{5}$

Here, you get the opposite conclusion, that Quantity B is greater than Quantity A. Because you can't arrive at a consistent conclusion, the answer is **(D)**.

Strategy Tip: The challenging part of this question was comparing the quantities after you had FOILed them. Notice you had to incorporate knowledge of positives and negatives to come to the correct conclusion. Harder questions will be difficult for either of two reasons:

1. Expressions are hard to FOIL, or
2. the comparisons are challenging.

Quadratics in Common Information

Questions that contain quadratic equations in the common information will present different challenges. For example:

$$x^2 - 6x + 8 = 0$$

Quantity A	**Quantity B**
x^2	2^x

The first thing to note here is that there will be two possible values for x. But you should not jump to conclusions and assume the answer will be (D). To make sure you get the right answer, you need to solve for both values of x and plug them *both* into the quantities.

First, solve for x by factoring the expression so that it reads $(x - 2)(x - 4) = 0$.

That means that $x = 2$ or $x = 4$. Start by plugging in 2 for x in both quantities:

Quantity A	**Quantity B**
$(2)^2 = \mathbf{4}$	$2^{(2)} = \mathbf{4}$

When $x = 2$, the quantities are equal.   A̶ B̶ C D

Now try $x = 4$:

Quantity A	**Quantity B**
$(4)^2 = \mathbf{16}$	$2^{(4)} = \mathbf{16}$

Even though there are two possible values for *x*, both of these values lead to the same conclusion: the quantities are equal. The correct answer is (C).

Strategy Tip: When the common information contains a quadratic equation, solve for *both* possible values and put them into the quantities.

Section Recap

There are two types of questions involving quadratics. Each type will require a different approach.

1. If a quadratic appears in one or both quantities:
    a. FOIL the quadratic,
    b. eliminate common terms, and
    c. compare the quantities.

2. If a quadratic appears in the common information:
    a. factor the equation and find *both* solutions, and
    b. plug both solutions into the quantities.

Formulas

Although relatively rare, strange symbol formulas do appear in Quantitative Comparison questions. The fastest way to answer them will depend on whether the question uses numbers or variables.

If you are given the numbers to plug into a strange symbol formula, you will need to evaluate the formula to answer the question. Refer to the *Algebra GRE Strategy Guide* for help on answering strange symbol formula questions.

If you're not given the numbers to plug in, the task is slightly different. For example:

$$v\& = 2v - 1$$

Quantity A   **Quantity B**

$(v\&)\&$ 4*v*

You could try plugging in different numbers, but you would have no way of knowing if the answer you got was always true. And trying multiple numbers would be tedious and time consuming. Instead, evaluate the formula using the variable itself. Start by evaluating the formula inside the parentheses:

$v\& = 2v - 1$

Rewrite Quantity A as $(2v - 1)\&$. Evaluate the formula one more time.

$(2v - 1)\& = 2(2v - 1) - 1$
$= 4v - 2 - 1$
$= 4v - 3$

Now your comparison looks like this:

Quantity A	**Quantity B**
$4v - 3$	$4v$
$\underline{-4v}$	$\underline{-4v}$
-3	0

Now, no matter what v is, Quantity B will be bigger.

By spending the time to evaluate the formula using the variable v, you can save time at the end of the problem. Once the formula was evaluated, a clear comparison could be made between the quantities.

Strategy Tip: There are two types of questions involving strange symbol formulas. Each type will require a different approach.

1. If the question contains numbers, plug in the numbers and evaluate the formula.

2. If the question does not contain numbers, plug the given variable(s) directly into the formula.

Inequalities & Absolute Values

Inequalities are a common theme in Quantitative Comparisons, and can take many forms. As was noted earlier in this section, one thing inequalities can do is restrict the range of a variable. Another way they are used is in combination with absolute values. For example:

$$-2 \le x \le 3$$
$$-3 \le y \le 2$$

Quantity A	**Quantity B**
The maximum value of $|x - 4|$	The maximum value of $|y + 4|$

Once again, inequalities are used to bound a variable. As before, you should test the **boundaries** of the range. But now, there's the added twist of absolute values. On QC, it is important to understand how to maximize and minimize values. The smallest possible value of any absolute value will be 0. *It is impossible for an absolute value to have a value less than 0.*

This question asks you to maximize the absolute values in Quantities A and B. In Quantity B, the maximum value of $|y + 4|$ will be when $y = 2$, because that is the largest number you can add to positive 4. The absolute value of $|y + 4|$ will equal 6.

To maximize the absolute value of $|x - 4|$ in Quantity A, however, you have to do the opposite. There is a negative 4 already in the absolute value. If you try to increase the value by adding a positive number to −4, you will only make the absolute value smaller. For instance, if x is 3, then the absolute value is:

$$|3 - 4| = |-1| = 1$$

You can actually maximize the absolute value by making $x = -2$. Then the absolute value becomes:

$$|-2 - 4| = |-6| = 6$$

Since the maximum value in each quantity is the same (6), the answer is **(C)**.

Strategy Tip: When absolute values contain a variable, **maximize** the absolute value by making the expression inside as far away from 0 as possible. Add positives to positives or add negatives to negatives.

Relative Order

The GRE often uses inequalities to show much more than the range of possible values for a variable. For instance, the common information may tell you that $0 < p < q < r$.

This inequality tells you two crucial things: 1) p, q, and r are all positive, and 2) p, q, and r are in order from least to greatest.

Questions that provide this type of information will often use different combinations of these variables in each quantity and perform some kind of mathematical operation on them (e.g., +, − , ×, ÷). You now have to **look for the pattern**.

If there is a pattern, the answer will be (A), (B), or (C). If there is no pattern, the answer will be (D). Make use of the Invisible Inequality to discern the pattern, if one is present. Take a look at four basic examples, one for each of the four basic mathematical operations (+, − , ×, ÷).

Example 1

$$0 < p < q < r$$

Quantity A   **Quantity B**

$p + q$ $q + r$

Pretend there is an unknown inequality between the two quantities, designated by a (?).

$$0 < p < q < r$$

| $p + q$ | (?) | $q + r$ |

Both sides contain a q, so subtract the q:

$$0 < p < q < r$$

Quantity A		**Quantity B**
$p + q$		$q + r$
$-q$	(?)	$-q$
p		r

3

From the common information ($0 < p < q < r$), you know that r is bigger than p, so Quantity B is definitely bigger.

Example 2

$$0 < p < q < r$$

Quantity A		**Quantity B**
pq	(?)	qr

Once again, both sides have a q. Because you know that q is positive, you can divide both sides by q without changing the Invisible Inequality:

$$0 < p < q < r$$

Quantity A		**Quantity B**
$\dfrac{pq}{q} = p$	(?)	$\dfrac{qr}{q} = r$

Once again, from the common information, you know that r is definitely greater than p. The correct answer is again (**B**).

In both of the last two examples, you were able to successfully eliminate common terms to arrive at a definite conclusion.

However, take a look at the next example.

Example 3

$$0 < p < q < r$$

Quantity A		**Quantity B**
$q - p$	(?)	$r - q$

Both sides contain a q, but notice that their signs are different. You can't actually eliminate q altogether. If you try adding q to both sides, here's what you get:

$$0 < p < q < r$$

Quantity A   **Quantity B**

$$\begin{array}{r} q - p \\ +q \\ \hline 2q - p \end{array} \qquad (?) \qquad \begin{array}{r} r - q \\ +q \\ \hline r \end{array}$$

Quantity A still contains q. Likewise, if you try subtracting q from both sides, you just push q into Quantity B:

$$0 < p < q < r$$

Quantity A   **Quantity B**

$$\begin{array}{r} q - p \\ -q \\ \hline -p \end{array} \qquad (?) \qquad \begin{array}{r} r - q \\ -q \\ \hline r - 2q \end{array}$$

Either way, you cannot arrive at a definite conclusion.

You can also pick numbers to show that there is no pattern. Remember to pick numbers satisfying $0 < p < q < r$. If $p = 1$, $q = 3$, and $r = 6$, then:

$$0 < p < q < r$$

Quantity A   **Quantity B**

$q - p = 3 - 1 = 2$ $\qquad (?) \qquad$ $r - q = 6 - 3 = 3$

With these numbers, Quantity B is bigger.   A̸B̸C̸D

Now space the numbers differently. In the previous case, q was closer to p than to r. Try putting q closer to r than to p.

If $p = 2$, $q = 7$, and $r = 8$, then:

$$0 < p < q < r$$

Quantity A   **Quantity B**

$q - p = 7 - 2 = 5$ $\qquad (?) \qquad$ $r - q = 8 - 7 = 1$

Now Quantity A is bigger. The correct answer is **(D)**.

There's a similar dilemma with this fourth example.

Example 4

$$0 < p < q < r$$

Quantity A		**Quantity B**
$\dfrac{q}{p}$	(?)	$\dfrac{r}{q}$

Because all the variables are positive, you can cross-multiply:

$$0 < p < q < r$$

Quantity A		**Quantity B**
q^2	(?)	pr

It's impossible to know for sure which quantity will be bigger. For extra practice, use numbers satisfying $0 < p < q < r$ to prove the answer is (D). (Hint: space the numbers differently, as in the example above.)

Strategy Tips: When absolute values contain variables, **maximize** the absolute value by making the expression inside as far away from 0 as possible.

1. If the absolute value also contains a positive number, make the variable positive to maximize the absolute value.

2. If the absolute value also contains a negative number, make the variable negative to maximize the absolute value.

Sometimes inequalities are used to order variables from least to greatest. In the previous examples, the common information ($0 < p < q < r$)

1. gave the sign of the variables, and

2. gave their order from least to greatest.

To compare the two quantities, use the Invisible Inequality to

1. eliminate common terms, and

2. try to discern a pattern if one is present.

Problem Set

1. $0 < x < 1$

Quantity A   **Quantity B**
$(x^3 - x)(4x + 3)$ $(x^2 + 1)(4x^2 + 3x)$

2. $6 \leq m \leq 12$

3

Quantity A   **Quantity B**
$9 - m$ $m - 9$

3.
$$\frac{\dfrac{-21}{2}m}{2} = \frac{7}{2}n$$

$$mn \neq 0$$

Quantity A   **Quantity B**
$3m$ $-n$

4.   **Quantity A**   **Quantity B**
     x $3x - 4$

5. $x^2 + x - 42 = 0$

Quantity A   **Quantity B**
$|x + 1|$ 5

6. $@(x) = x^2 - 4$

Quantity A	**Quantity B**
$@(10)$	$@(@(4))$

7. $\clubsuit x = \dfrac{1}{x-1}$

Quantity A	**Quantity B**
$\clubsuit(\clubsuit x)$	$\dfrac{x-1}{2-x}$

8. $|x - 2| > 3$

Quantity A	**Quantity B**
The minimum possible value of $|x - 3.5|$	The minimum possible value of $|x - 1.5|$

9. $a < b < 0 < c < d$

Quantity A	**Quantity B**
abc	$c - d$

10. $0 < a < 1 < b < c$

Quantity A	**Quantity B**
$\dfrac{c^2}{a}$	$\dfrac{bc}{ab}$

MANHATTAN
PREP

Answer Key

1. (B) 2. (D) 3. (D) 4. (D) 5. (A) 6. (B) 7. (C) 8. (B) 9. (A) 10. (A)

Solutions

3

1. **(B):** Notice that in each of the quantities, you can factor an x out of one of the expressions:

$$0 < x < 1$$

Quantity A	**Quantity B**
$(x^3 - x)(4x + 3) =$	$(x^2 + 1)(4x^2 + 3x) =$
$x(x^2 - 1)(4x + 3)$	$(x^2 + 1)(4x + 3)x$

Because you know that x is not 0, you can use the Invisible Inequality to divide away the common terms from both quantities (x and $(4x + 3)$):

$$0 < x < 1$$

Quantity A	**Quantity B**
$x(x^2 - 1)(4x + 3) =$	$(x^2 + 1)(4x + 3)x =$
$x^2 - 1$	$x^2 + 1$

Now the comparison is easy to make. Because x^2 will always be positive, $(x^2 + 1)$ will always be bigger than $(x^2 - 1)$.

2. **(D):** Try to prove (D) by testing the boundaries of the range for m.

If $m = 6$, then Quantity A is equal to $9 - (6) = 3$, and Quantity B is equal to $(6) - 9 = -3$. Eliminate answer choices (B) and (C).

If $m = 12$, then Quantity A is equal to $9 - (12) = -3$, and Quantity B is equal to $(12) - 9 = 3$. Eliminate answer choice (A).

The answer is (D).

3. **(D):** Never leave a complex fraction in place; that is, simplify in order to find a direct comparison. First, multiply both sides by 2:

$$\frac{\dfrac{-21}{2}m}{2} = \frac{7}{2}n \quad \rightarrow \quad \frac{-21}{2}m = 7n$$

Multiply both sides by 2 again:

$$\frac{-21}{2}m = 7n \quad \rightarrow \quad -21m = 14n$$

Divide by −7 in order to make the left side of the equation $3m$ (Quantity A):

$$-21m = 14n \quad \rightarrow \quad 3m = -2n$$

Since $3m = -2n$, you can substitute $-2n$ for $3m$ in Quantity A. The problem now reads:

$$mn \neq 0$$

Quantity A	**Quantity B**
$-2n$	$-n$

If n is positive, Quantity B is bigger. If n is negative, Quantity A is bigger.

The answer is (D).

4. **(D):** If there are no constraints on a variable, try to prove (D).

If $x = 0$, Quantity A is equal to 0 and Quantity B is equal to −4. Eliminate answer choices (B) and (C). If $x = 10$, Quantity A is equal to 10 and Quantity B is equal to 26. Eliminate answer choice (A).

The answer is (D).

5. **(A):** This question contains a quadratic equation in the common information. The first thing to note here is that there will be two possible values for x. But you should not jump to conclusions and assume the answer will be (D). To make sure you get the right answer, solve for both values of x and plug them BOTH into the quantities:

$$x^2 + x - 42 = 0$$
$$(x + 7)(x - 6) = 0$$
$$x = -7 \text{ or } 6$$

Now the problem reads:

$$x = -7 \text{ or } 6$$

Quantity A	**Quantity B**
$|x + 1|$	5

If $x = -7$, Quantity A is equal to the absolute value of −6, which is 6, and Quantity B will still be equal to 5. If $x = 6$, Quantity A is equal to the absolute value of 7, which is 7, and Quantity B will still be equal to 5.

In either case, Quantity A is bigger.

MANHATTAN
PREP

6. (B): If a QC question with a strange symbol formula contains numbers, *plug in* the numbers and evaluate the formula.

In Quantity A, $@(10) = (10)^2 - 4 = 96$.

In Quantity B, work outwards from the "inner core." $@(4) = 4^2 - 4 = 12$. Now evaluate $@(12)$.

$@(12) = 12^2 - 4 = 140$.

Quantity B is bigger.

The answer is (B).

3

7. (C): Remember, if you are given a strange symbol on the GRE, the exam will have to define that strange symbol for you. Since you are not given numbers to plug in, you should evaluate the formula using the variable itself—otherwise, if you plugged in numbers, you would have no way of knowing whether you would have to try more numbers to try to prove (D).

Quantity A asks for ♣(♣x). They want you to plug the function into itself. So, plug $\dfrac{1}{x-1}$ in for x:

$$\cfrac{1}{\cfrac{1}{x-1}-1}$$

Combine the two terms in the denominator:

$$\cfrac{1}{\cfrac{1}{x-1}-1} \quad \rightarrow \quad \cfrac{1}{\cfrac{1}{x-1}-\cfrac{x-1}{x-1}} = \cfrac{1}{\cfrac{2-x}{x-1}}$$

Remember, if a fraction is under a 1, just flip it over:

$$\cfrac{1}{\cfrac{2-x}{x-1}} = \frac{x-1}{2-x}$$

The answer is (C).

8. (B): As with all absolute value equations or inequalities, here you must solve twice:

$$|x-2| > 3$$
$$x - 2 > 3 \qquad or \qquad x - 2 < -3$$
$$x > 5 \qquad or \qquad x < -1$$

Even better, you could express the possible values of *x* on a number line:

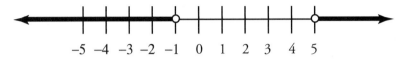

Quantity A is equal to the minimum possible value of $|x - 3.5|$. Another way to think of $|x - 3.5|$ is the distance on a number line from *x* to 3.5. Look at 3.5 on the number line above and note the nearest possible distance that is greater than 5 (*x* may not be exactly 5, but it could be 5.000001, for instance, since there is no requirement that it be an integer). Therefore, since the distance from 3.5 to greater than 5 is greater than 1.5, Quantity A is equal to greater than 1.5. That is, the minimum possible value of $|x - 3.5|$ is 1.5 plus any very small amount—for instance, 1.5000001 would be a legal value.

Quantity B can be conceived as the smallest distance from *x* to 1.5. Look at 1.5 on the number line—the nearest value is less than −1, which is more than 2.5 units away. Thus, the minimum possible value of $|x - 1.5|$ is greater than 2.5.

If Quantity A's minimum is just greater than 1.5 and Quantity B's minimum is just greater than 2.5, Quantity B is larger.

The answer is (B).

You could also solve this problem by plugging in values, rather than using a number line. First, solve the inequality as above to get $x > 5$ or $x < -1$. Now try plugging in greater than 5, less than −1, as well as very small and very large numbers—that is, the extremes of both ranges for *x* (although you may be able to use a bit of logic beforehand to tell that you only want values very close to 1.5 and 3.5)—to make sure that you generate the smallest possible value for each quantity. Quantity A's smallest value will be smaller than Quantity B's smallest value.

The answer is (B).

9. **(A):** When variables are ordered from least to greatest, **look for the pattern**. Notice that *a* and *b* are negative, and *c* and *d* are positive. Try working only with positives and negatives first, before considering more specific numbers.

In Quantity A, *abc* is a negative times a negative times a positive—that is, Quantity A is a positive value.

In Quantity B, $c - d$ is a positive minus a positive. Now, a positive minus a positive can yield either a positive or a negative value (for instance 10 minus 1 versus 1 minus 10). So look back up at the common information to see that *d* is greater than *c*. Thus, $c - d$ is an instance of subtracting a larger positive from a smaller positive, which yields a negative.

Quantity A is positive and Quantity B is negative.

The answer is (A).

10. **(A):** When variables are ordered from least to greatest, look for the pattern. You can also use the technique of the invisible inequality—and since all of the variables are positive, you can cross-multiply across that invisible inequality:

$$\frac{c^2}{a} \qquad ? \qquad \frac{bc}{ab}$$

$$abc^2 \qquad ? \qquad abc$$

Since you know a, b, and c are positive, go ahead and divide out abc:

$$c \qquad ? \qquad 1$$

You were directly told in the common information that $1 < c$, so Quantity A is bigger.

The answer is (A).

Chapter 4

of

Quantitative Comparisons
& Data Interpretation

Fractions, Decimals,
& Percents

In This Chapter...

Chapter 4
Fractions, Decimals, & Percents

Fractions are ubiquitous on the GRE, and you will need a variety of skills to deal with them properly. This chapter outlines some of the more common strategies you can employ to save time and get questions right. Again, you should expect to practice these strategies multiple times before you can consistently and naturally apply them.

Quick Elimination: Less Than 1 vs. Greater Than 1

Sometimes answering a question is as simple as asking, "Is this fraction greater than or less than 1?" To answer this question, you just have to compare the numerator and the denominator:

$$n > 0$$

Quantity A	**Quantity B**
$\dfrac{n}{n+1}$	$\dfrac{n+1}{n}$

If n is positive, then so is $n + 1$. Both fractions have positive numerators and denominators. Now you can ask, "Is $\dfrac{n}{n+1}$ greater than or less than 1?" Since $n + 1$ is bigger than n, you can quickly see that $\dfrac{n}{n+1}$ is less than 1. Likewise, you can quickly see that $\dfrac{n+1}{n}$ is greater than 1. The correct answer is

(B).

Strategy Tip: It only takes a few seconds to ask whether each fraction is greater than or less than 1. If this approach works, you have saved yourself time. If it does not work, you have only spent a few seconds and can quickly move to a new approach.

Simplifying Complex Fractions

Occasionally, a Quantitative Comparison (QC) has a complex fraction in one or both of the quantities. A complex fraction is any fraction that has a fraction in either the numerator or the denominator. For example:

$$x > 0$$

Quantity A	**Quantity B**
$\dfrac{2+\dfrac{2}{3x}}{2}$	$\dfrac{3+\dfrac{3}{2x}}{3}$

A good first step is to SPLIT THE NUMERATOR:

$$x > 0$$

Quantity A	**Quantity B**
$\dfrac{2+\dfrac{2}{3x}}{2} =$	$\dfrac{3+\dfrac{3}{2x}}{3} =$
$\dfrac{2}{2}+\dfrac{\dfrac{2}{3x}}{2}$	$\dfrac{3}{3}+\dfrac{\dfrac{3}{2x}}{3}$

Splitting the numerator is helpful because the denominator is just one term. Now it is easy to see that both quantities contain a 1 (2/2 and 3/3 both equal 1). You then can subtract 1 from both quantities, because of the Invisible Inequality:

$$x > 0$$

Quantity A		**Quantity B**
$\dfrac{2}{2}+\dfrac{\dfrac{2}{3x}}{2} =$	?	$\dfrac{3}{3}+\dfrac{\dfrac{3}{2x}}{3} =$
$\dfrac{\dfrac{2}{3x}}{2}$		$\dfrac{\dfrac{3}{2x}}{3}$

Now you need to focus on the complex fractions in each quantity. The next step is to divide both fractions Remember: fraction bars represent division. Also keep straight which is the "big" fraction bar:

$$\dfrac{\dfrac{3}{2x}}{3} \neq \dfrac{3}{\dfrac{2x}{3}}$$

One way to divide is to multiply by the reciprocal. The numerator of the fraction in Quantity A is being divided by 2. That is the same as multiplying by the reciprocal of 2, which is $\dfrac{1}{2}$. You can do something similar with the fraction in Quantity B:

$$x > 0$$

Quantity A	**Quantity B**
$\dfrac{\dfrac{2}{3x}}{2} =$	$\dfrac{\dfrac{3}{2x}}{3} =$
$\dfrac{2}{3x} \cdot \dfrac{1}{2}$	$\dfrac{3}{2x} \cdot \dfrac{1}{3}$

Now you can simplify the expressions:

$$x > 0$$

Quantity A	**Quantity B**
$\dfrac{\cancel{2}}{3x} \cdot \dfrac{1}{\cancel{2}} =$	$\dfrac{\cancel{3}}{2x} \cdot \dfrac{1}{\cancel{3}} =$
$\dfrac{1}{3x}$	$\dfrac{1}{2x}$

Remember, as a positive denominator gets larger, the fraction gets smaller. Since $x > 0$, the denominator of $\dfrac{1}{3x}$ will always be bigger than the denominator of $\dfrac{1}{2x}$. Therefore, the fraction in Quantity B will always be larger. Answer choice **(B)** is the correct answer.

Strategy Tip: When simplifying complex fractions, look to:

1. SPLIT THE NUMERATOR when the denominator is one term, and
2. turn division into multiplication by the reciprocal $\left(\text{e.g., } \dfrac{2}{2/3} = 2 \cdot \dfrac{3}{2} \right)$.

Fractions with Exponents—Plug In 0 and 1

Fractions containing exponents are challenging, but they can also present opportunities to save some time. For example:

Quantity A	**Quantity B**
$\dfrac{1}{2^t}$	2^t

The first step is to plug in numbers. To save yourself time, always try the numbers 0 and 1 first (unless the common information rules out those values, such as by specifying that a variable is negative). Anything raised to the 0th power equals 1 (e.g., $2^0 = 1$). Anything raised to the 1st power equals itself.

If you plug in 0 for t, then the quantities are:

Quantity A	Quantity B
$\dfrac{1}{2^0} = \dfrac{1}{1} = 1$	$2^0 = 1$

When $t = 0$, the quantities are equal.   A̶ B̶ C D

Now plug in 1:

Quantity A	Quantity B
$\dfrac{1}{2^1} = \dfrac{1}{2}$	$2^1 = 2$

Now Quantity B is bigger. The correct answer is **(D)**.

Strategy Tip: When fractions contain exponents and you have to plug in numbers for the exponents, always plug in 0 and 1 first to save yourself time.

Percents

The Original Value

An important consideration when dealing with percents is the size of the total that you are taking a percent of. For example:

An item is discounted by 20%, and then a 20% surcharge is applied to the discounted price.

Quantity A	Quantity B
The price after the discount and surcharge	The original price

Two percent operations are performed. First, a price is discounted by 20%. The new price is now 80% of the original. Next, 20% is added to this new price. Two things are important to note here:

1. The percent increase (as a *percentage*) is the same as the percent decrease, and

2. the percent increase is based on the NEW, smaller price.

In dollar terms, the 20% increase will have to be smaller than the original 20% decrease, because you are adding 20% to a smaller number. Without any actual calculations, you can be confident that the price after the discount and the surcharge will be less than the original price.

You can also demonstrate this principle by picking a price for the item. As always, a good number to use when you work with percents is 100.

The 20% discount is 20% of **100** = 0.2 × 100 = $20.

The new price is $100 − $20 = $80.

The 20% surcharge is 20% of **80** = 0.2 × 80 = $16. Use the calculator for this if you need to.

The final price is $80 + $16 = $96.

The original price ($100) is larger than the final price after the discount and surcharge ($96). The answer is **(B)**.

4

Strategy Tip: When dealing with percents, always pay attention to the size of the original value. Thus, 20% of a small number is less than 20% of a larger number.

Problem Set

1. A town's population rose 40% from 2006 to 2007.
    The 2007 population was 10,080.

Quantity A	**Quantity B**
The 2006 population	7,000

2. | **Quantity A** | **Quantity B** |
    |---|---|
    | $\dfrac{1}{3}+\dfrac{1}{4}+\dfrac{7}{12}$ | $\dfrac{1}{\dfrac{1}{3}+\dfrac{1}{4}+\dfrac{7}{12}}$ |

3. | **Quantity A** | **Quantity B** |
    |---|---|
    | $\dfrac{1}{6}-\left(\dfrac{1}{2}\right)^2+\left(-\dfrac{1}{4}\right)^2$ | $\dfrac{1}{6}$ |

4. | **Quantity A** | **Quantity B** |
    |---|---|
    | $\dfrac{\dfrac{4}{3}+(-2)}{-2}$ | $\dfrac{-\dfrac{4}{3}+2}{2}$ |

5. $x > 1$

Quantity A	**Quantity B**
$\dfrac{x+5}{x}$	$\dfrac{(x-1)+5}{x-1}$

6.

$$x = -y$$
$$xy \neq 0$$

Quantity A	**Quantity B**
$\dfrac{5.5x^2}{5}$	$\dfrac{3y^2}{2.5}$

7.

Quantity A	**Quantity B**
$(0.\overline{7})(0.8)(35)$	$(1.8)(15)(0.\overline{7})$

8.

A particular rent price increased x% from 2003 to 2004.
The rent then decreased by x% from 2004 to 2005.
x is a positive integer.

Quantity A	**Quantity B**
The difference between 2004's price and 2003's price, in dollars	The difference between 2004's price and 2005's price, in dollars

9.

$$m = 120\% \text{ of } n$$

Quantity A	**Quantity B**
$\dfrac{6}{5}n$	$\dfrac{5}{6}m$

10.

Quantity A	**Quantity B**
$0.125 + \dfrac{4}{5} + \dfrac{2}{3} + 1.2$	$0.8 + 0.\overline{6} + \dfrac{6}{5} + \dfrac{1}{8}$

Answer Key

1. (A)   2. (A)   3. (B)   4. (C)   5. (B)   6. (B)   7. (A)   8. (B)   9. (D)   10. (C)

Solutions

1. **(A):** The common information tells you that the 2006 population rose by 40% to a population of 10,080. If x is the population in 2006, then written as math, that's $1.4x = 10,080$.

Warning: You may **not** simply take away 40% of 10,080. This will yield an incorrect answer. Why? The 40% increase is 40% *of the 2006 population,* not 40% of the 2007 population. To calculate that, you need the equation $1.4x = 10,080$.

So, $x = \dfrac{10,080}{1.4} = 7,200$, which is greater than 7,000.

Alternatively, you could use Quantity B as a benchmark.

What if the original population had been 7,000? Raise *that* by 40%. One fast way to increase by 40% is to multiply by 1.4, rather than multiplying by 0.4 to generate the 40% and then adding it back on to the original number:

$$\begin{array}{r} 1.4 \\ \times\,7,000 \\ \hline 9,800.0 \end{array}$$

That is, if the 2006 population had been 7,000, the 2007 population would have been 9,800. Since the population was actually 10,080, you know that the original population must have been higher than 7,000.

The answer is (A).

2. **(A):** Compare, don't calculate. It is not necessary to solve this problem, just to note that $\dfrac{1}{3} + \dfrac{1}{4} + \dfrac{7}{12}$ is greater than 1. How do you know that? Well, $\dfrac{7}{12}$ is more than half already, $\dfrac{1}{4} + \dfrac{1}{4}$ would be another half, and $\dfrac{1}{3}$ is more than $\dfrac{1}{4}$. Thus, is $\dfrac{1}{3} + \dfrac{1}{4}$ more than half?

In Quantity A, "more than half" plus "more than half" is "more than 1."
In Quantity B, dividing 1 by "more than 1" is "less than 1."

The answer is (A).

3. **(B):** This is another "compare, don't calculate" problem. Since $\frac{1}{6}$ is present on both sides, simply subtract it:

Quantity A	**Quantity B**
$\frac{1}{6} - \left(\frac{1}{2}\right)^2 + \left(-\frac{1}{4}\right)^2$	$\frac{1}{6}$
$-\left(\frac{1}{2}\right)^2 + \left(-\frac{1}{4}\right)^2$	0

Now you only have to determine whether $-\left(\frac{1}{2}\right)^2 + \left(-\frac{1}{4}\right)^2$ is negative, positive, or 0:

$$-\left(\frac{1}{2}\right)^2 + \left(-\frac{1}{4}\right)^2 = -\frac{1}{4} + \frac{1}{16}$$

Since $-\frac{1}{4} + \frac{1}{16}$ is definitely still negative, no further calculation is needed.

The answer is (B).

4. **(C):** The calculator might be tempting here, but there's a faster way. These quantities can both be simplified quickly if you split the numerator of each fraction:

Quantity A	**Quantity B**
$\dfrac{\frac{4}{3} + (-2)}{-2} =$	$\dfrac{-\frac{4}{3} + 2}{2} =$
$\dfrac{\frac{4}{3}}{-2} + \dfrac{-2}{-2}$	$\dfrac{\frac{-4}{3}}{2} + \dfrac{2}{2}$

Since $-2/-2$ and $2/2$ are each equal to 1, cancel them out from each side:

Quantity A	**Quantity B**
$\dfrac{\frac{4}{3}}{-2}$	$\dfrac{\frac{4}{3}}{-2}$

On both sides, you have $\frac{4}{3}$ divided by 2, with a single negative sign. When working with fractions, it doesn't matter whether a negative sign is with the numerator, with the denominator, or out front—for example, $\frac{-1}{2}$, $\frac{1}{-2}$, and $-\frac{1}{2}$ are all equal. Don't bother to simplify either quantity.

The answer is (C).

5. (B): This is another problem for which you can split the numerator of each fraction:

<table>
<tr><td align="center"><u>**Quantity A**</u></td><td align="center">$x > 1$</td><td align="center"><u>**Quantity B**</u></td></tr>
<tr><td align="center">$\dfrac{x+5}{x} = \dfrac{x}{x} + \dfrac{5}{x}$</td><td></td><td align="center">$\dfrac{(x-1)+5}{x-1} = \dfrac{x-1}{x-1} + \dfrac{5}{x-1}$</td></tr>
</table>

Since $\dfrac{x}{x}$ and $\dfrac{x-1}{x-1}$ are each equal to 1, cancel them out from both sides:

<table>
<tr><td align="center"><u>**Quantity A**</u></td><td align="center"><u>**Quantity B**</u></td></tr>
<tr><td align="center">$\dfrac{5}{x}$</td><td align="center">$\dfrac{5}{x-1}$</td></tr>
</table>

You know x is a positive number greater than 1. So remember: *as the denominator gets larger, the fraction gets smaller.* Thus, Quantity B, which has the smaller denominator, is the larger fraction.

The answer is (B).

6. (B): You are told that $x = -y$ and that neither one is 0; that is, the two numbers are inverses of one another (such as 2 and −2). However, when both are squared, the negative one becomes positive and the two values become equal. $x^2 = y^2$, so you can simply divide out x^2 and y^2 to get:

<table>
<tr><td align="center"><u>**Quantity A**</u></td><td align="center"><u>**Quantity B**</u></td></tr>
<tr><td align="center">$\dfrac{5.5}{5}$</td><td align="center">$\dfrac{3}{2.5}$</td></tr>
</table>

Although the fractions have different denominators, you can very easily convert to a common denominator of 5. Multiply the fraction in Quantity B by $\dfrac{2}{2}$:

<table>
<tr><td align="center"><u>**Quantity A**</u></td><td align="center"><u>**Quantity B**</u></td></tr>
<tr><td align="center">$\dfrac{5.5}{5}$</td><td align="center">$\dfrac{3}{2.5} \times \dfrac{2}{2} = \dfrac{6}{5}$</td></tr>
</table>

The fraction in Quantity B is greater.

7. (A): First, divide the common element $(0.\overline{7})$ from each side to get:

<table>
<tr><td align="center"><u>**Quantity A**</u></td><td align="center"><u>**Quantity B**</u></td></tr>
<tr><td align="center">$(0.8)(35)$</td><td align="center">$(1.8)(15)$</td></tr>
</table>

Now, it's a calculator workout:

$$(0.8)(35) = 28$$
$$(1.8)(15) = 27$$

The answer is (A).

8. **(B):** An important consideration in dealing with percents is the size of the total. You don't know 2003's rent price, but you do know that 2004's—after the increase—is higher.

When the rent increases from 2003 to 2004, it goes up *x% of 2003's price.*
When the rent decreases from 2004 to 2005, it goes down *x% of 2004's price.*

Since 2004's price is higher than 2003's price, the second change is a greater dollar figure. That is, both changes are *x*%, but the second change is *x*% of a larger number, and hence a larger change in dollars. Quantity B's figure is greater.

You could also demonstrate this with numbers. Say 2003's price is $100 and *x* = 10. Thus:

2003 = $100
2004 = $110
2005 = $99

The difference between 2004 and 2005 is greater than the difference between 2004 and 2003.

The answer is (B).

9. **(D):** Converting 120% to fraction form will help simplify. 120% is equivalent to $\frac{6}{5}$. Rewrite the common information as $m = \frac{6}{5}n$. Now substitute $\frac{6}{5}n$ in place of *m* in Quantity B:

Quantity A	**Quantity B**
$\frac{6}{5}n$	$\frac{5}{6}m = \frac{5}{6}\left(\frac{6}{5}n\right)$

Thus, Quantity A is equal to $\frac{6}{5}n$ and Quantity B is simply equal to $n\left(\frac{5}{6} \times \frac{6}{5} = 1\right)$. It would seem that Quantity A is greater—however, what if *n* is negative? For example, if *n* is −1, Quantity A would be −1.2 and Quantity B would be −1, making Quantity B greater.

The answer is (D).

MANHATTAN
PREP

10. **(C):** Use percent benchmarks to compare quantities, and cancel common elements. (The repeating decimal should be a clue that you are not really required to add all those quantities).

$0.125 = \dfrac{1}{8}$, so cancel 0.125 from Quantity A and $\dfrac{1}{8}$ from Quantity B.

$\dfrac{4}{5} = 0.8$, so cancel $\dfrac{4}{5}$ from Quantity A and 0.8 from Quantity B.

$\dfrac{2}{3} = 0.\overline{6}$, so cancel $\dfrac{2}{3}$ from Quantity A and $0.\overline{6}$ from Quantity B.

The last remaining quantities, 1.2 and $\dfrac{6}{5}$, are also equal. The two quantities are equal.

The answer is (C).

Alternatively, use the calculator! One of the nice things about the on-screen calculator is that it respects order of operations. In other words, just key in the formula:

$$0.125 + 4 \div 5 + 2 \div 3 + 1.2 =$$

And you'll get 2.7917 for Quantity A.

Now the same for Quantity B:

$$0.8 + 0.6667 + 6 \div 5 + 1 \div 8 =$$

And you'll get 2.7917.

The answer is (C).

4

Chapter 5

of

Quantitative Comparisons
& Data Interpretation

Geometry

In This Chapter...

Chapter 5
Geometry

This chapter is different from the others. The other topic chapters (Algebra, Fractions, Decimals, Percents, Number Properties, and Word Problems) are broken down into content areas (exponents, quadratic equations, etc.). This chapter provides a more general approach for Geometry questions, classified not by content area (e.g., Circles, Polygons), but by format.

Success on Geometry Quantitative Comparison (QC) questions will still be largely determined by your knowledge of the rules and formulas associated with all the shapes tested on the GRE. This chapter offers a practical approach to correctly applying these rules and formulas to *every* QC question, regardless of the shape or shapes being tested.

This chapter is broken down as follows:

1. How to deal with **Shape Geometry** questions that include a diagram:

   A. What to do when Quantity B contains a number.

   B. What to do when Quantity B contains an unknown, such as a variable or an angle shown in the diagram.

2. How to deal with **Word Geometry** questions that do *not* include a diagram.

The following three-step process for tackling Geometry QC questions will be emphasized:

1. Establish what you **need to know**.

2. Establish what you **know**.

3. Establish what you **don't know**.

Shape Geometry

Quantity B Is a NUMBER

The most straightforward Geometry Quantitative Comparison problems are ones in which you are given the diagram and Quantity B is a number. You can attack these with the basic three-step process outlined earlier. In most cases, you should quickly redraw the diagram you are given. Avoid the temptation simply to look and solve, since you could easily make mistakes.

On Geometry QCs, as on all QCs, there is always the possibility that you will not have enough information, resulting in a correct answer of (D). However, to arrive at the correct answer consistently, you must *act as though there is enough information, while accepting that the answer may ultimately be (D)*. For example:

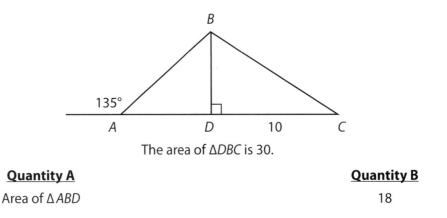

The area of △*DBC* is 30.

Quantity A	**Quantity B**
Area of △*ABD*	18

For any Geometry QC problem, the first step is the same: establish what you **need to know**.

Quantity B is a number, so no calculations are necessary.

Quantity A is the area of triangle *ABD*. This is the value you need to know. For any value you need to know, there are three possible scenarios:

    1. You can find an exact value.

    2. You can find a range of possible values.

    3. You do not have enough information to find the value.

Approach every Geometry QC as if you will be able to find an exact value, but recognize that you won't always be able to.

Now that you have established what you need to know, it is time to establish what you **know**.

To figure out what you know, use the given information to find values for previously unknown lengths and angles. You will do this by setting up equations and making inferences.

Keywords such as *area, perimeter,* and *circumference* are good indications that you can set up equations to solve for a previously unknown length. In this example, the area of triangle *DBC* is given. First, write the general formula for the area of a triangle, and then plug in all the known values:

$$\text{Area}_{\triangle DBC} = \frac{1}{2}(b)(h)$$

The area is given as 30, and line segment *DC* is the base of the triangle:

$$30 = \frac{1}{2}(10)(h)$$

Isolate *h* to solve for the height of the triangle:

$$30 = \frac{1}{2}(10)(h)$$

$$30 = 5h$$

$$6 = h$$

Immediately add any new information to your diagram:

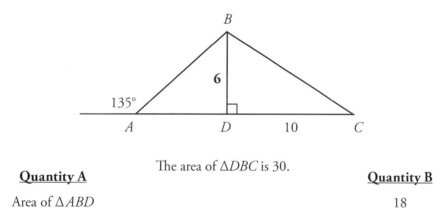

The area of △*DBC* is 30.

Quantity A	**Quantity B**
Area of △*ABD*	18

Now that the length of *BD* is known, you *could* use the Pythagorean Theorem to calculate the length of *BC*. However, *keep the end in mind as you work*. Knowing the length of *BC* won't tell you anything about triangle *ABD*, so save time by focusing on other pieces of the diagram.

At this stage, no other lengths can be calculated (apart from *BC*). Now ask yourself, "Are there any equations I can set up to find new angles?"

In general, you will find new angles with formulas that involve sums. Key features of diagrams include intersecting lines with one known angle, parallel lines with a transversal and one known angle, and triangles with two known angles:

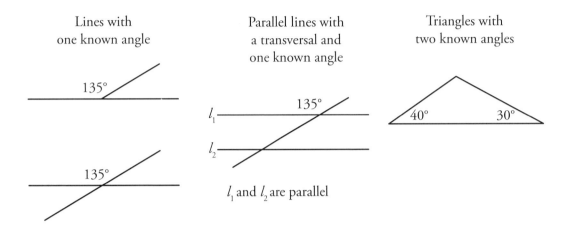

In this diagram, you have lines with a known angle. Line segment AB divides the horizontal line into two parts. Straight lines have a degree measure of 180°, so set up an equation:

$$135° + \angle BAD = 180°$$
$$\angle BAD = 45°$$

Put 45° on your copy of the diagram. Use the calculator for this sort of computation, if need be. Once you get fast, you can do the computation in your head, but you should always add it to the picture.

By the same logic, you also know that $\angle BDA = 90$:

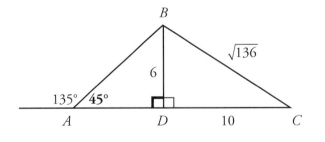

The area of $\triangle DBC$ is 30.

Quantity A	**Quantity B**
Area of $\triangle ABD$	18

Now two of the angles in triangle *ABD* are known. You can solve for the third angle:

$$90° + 45° + \angle ABD = 180°$$
$$135° + \angle ABD = 180°$$
$$\angle ABD = 45°$$

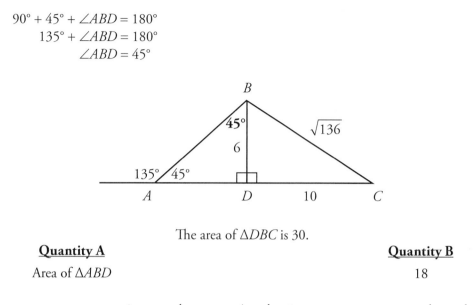

The area of △*DBC* is 30.

Quantity A   **Quantity B**

Area of △*ABD*   18

At this stage, no more equations can be set up. Another important component when solving Geometry QC problems is *making inferences*. Not everything you learn will come from equations. Rather, special properties of shapes and relationships between shapes will allow you to make inferences.

In this diagram, $\angle BAD$ and $\angle ABD$ both lie in triangle *ABD* and have a degree measure of 45°. That means that triangle *ABD* is isosceles, and that the sides opposite $\angle BAD$ and $\angle ABD$ are equal. Side *BD* has a length of 6, which means side *AD* also has a length of 6:

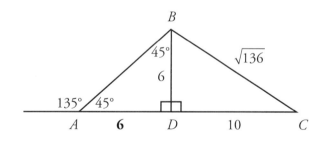

The area of △*DBC* is 30.

Quantity A   **Quantity B**

Area of △*ABD*   18

Remember that the value you need to know is the area of triangle *ABD*. There is now sufficient information in the diagram to find that value. *AD* is the base and *BD* is the height. Thus:

$$\text{Area}_{\triangle ABD} = \frac{1}{2}(6)(6) = 18$$

The values in the two quantities are equal and the answer is (**C**).

Strategy Tip: Many QCs will provide enough information to reach a definite conclusion. To solve for the value you **need to know**:

<u>Establish What You Know</u>

1. *Set up equations* to find the values of previously unknown *lines* and *angles*.
2. *Make inferences* to find additional information.

<u>Establish What You Don't Know</u>

While many questions provide you enough information, you will not always be able to find an exact number for the value you need. For these questions, an additional step will be required: establish what you don't know.

Even though you will not always be able to find the exact value of something you need to know, implicit constraints within a diagram will often provide you a range of possible values. You will need to identify this range:

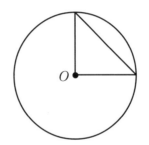

The circle with center *O*
has an area of 4*π*.

Quantity A   **Quantity B**

Area of the triangle   1.5

First, establish what you **need to know**. To find the area of the triangle, you will need the base and the height.

Now, establish what you **know**. The area of the circle is 4*π*, and Area = *πr²*, so:

$$4\pi = \pi r^2$$
$$4 = r^2$$
$$2 = r$$

MANHATTAN
PREP

The radius equals 2. Two lines in the diagram are radii. Label these radii:

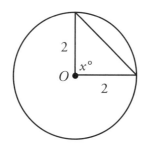

The circle with center O
has an area of 4π.

Quantity A   **Quantity B**

Area of the triangle   1.5

Now the question becomes, "Is there enough information to find the area of the triangle?"

Be careful! Remember, *don't trust the picture*. The triangle in the diagram appears to be a right triangle. If that were the case, then the radii could act as the base and the height of the triangle, and the area would be:

$$\text{Area} = \frac{1}{2}(b)(h) = \frac{1}{2}(2)(2) = 2$$

The answer would be (A). But there is one problem—the diagram does not provide any information about x.

Of course, you do know a few things about the angle. Because x is one angle in a triangle, it has an implicit range: it must be greater than 0° and less than 180°.

x is a value you **don't know**. The question now becomes, "How do changes to x affect the area of the triangle?" To find out, take the unknown value (x) to extremes.

You know what the area of the triangle is when $x = 90°$. What happens as x increases?

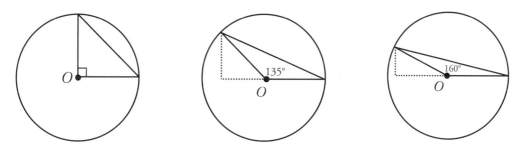

As x increases, the height of the triangle decreases, and thus the area of the triangle decreases as well.

In fact, as *x* gets closer and closer to its maximum value, the height gets closer and closer to 0. As the height gets closer to 0, so does the area of the triangle.

In other words:

$$0 < \text{area of triangle} \leq 2$$

Compare this range to Quantity B. The area of the triangle can be either greater than or less than 1.5. The correct answer is **(D)**.

Strategy Tip: On some Geometry QC questions, it will be impossible to find an exact value for the value you need. After you have established what you **need to know** and established what you KNOW, you have to establish what you **don't know**.

For values that you don't know, take them to extremes and see how these changes affect the value you need to know.

Quantity B Is an Unknown Value

This section is about some of the situations you will encounter when both quantities contain *unknown values*.

The basic process remains the same:

1. Establish what you **need to know**.

2. Establish what you **know**.

3. Establish what you **don't know**.

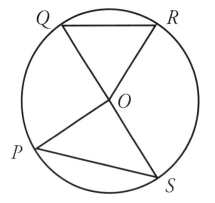

O is the center of the circle.
∠*QOR* > ∠*POS*

Quantity A	**Quantity B**
minor arc *QR*	minor arc *PS*

The first step, establish what you **need to know**, is now more complicated, because there are two unknown values: Quantity A *and* Quantity B.

When both quantities contain an unknown, you need to know *either* the values in both quantities *or*, more likely, the relative size of the two values. For this problem, you will need to either solve for minor arcs *QR* and *PS* or determine their relative size.

Now, establish what you **know**. Remember: Don't trust the picture! The way the diagram is drawn, *PS* appears larger than *QR*. That means nothing.

Actually, there is not a whole lot to know—no actual numbers have been given. *OP, OQ, OR,* and *OS* are radii, and thus have equal lengths. Other than that, the only thing you know is that ∠*QOR* > ∠*POS*.

With no numbers provided in the question, finding exact values for either quantity is out of the question. But you may still be able to say something definite about their *relative size.*

Now, establish what you **don't know**. What values in the diagram are unknown and can affect the lengths of *QR* and *PS*? ∠*QOR* and ∠*POS* fulfill both criteria. Take the values of ∠*QOR* and ∠*POS* to extremes.

How do changes to ∠*QOR* and ∠*POS* affect the lengths of *QR* and *PS*?

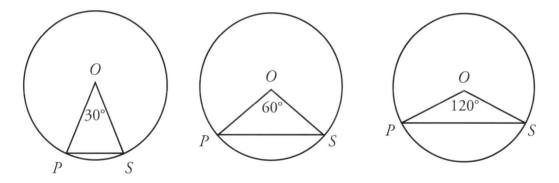

Note that you do not need specific angle measures in these examples—rough sketches will do.

As ∠*POS* gets bigger, so does minor arc *PS*. You can assume the same relationship is true in triangle *QOR*.

Because *OP = OQ = OR = OS*, you can directly compare the two triangles. ∠*QOR* > ∠*POS*, which means that no matter what the values of ∠*QOR* and ∠*POS* actually are, minor arc *QR* is definitely greater than minor arc *PS*. The correct answer is **(A)**.

Strategy Tip: When QC questions include a diagram, there are two possibilities for Quantity B:

1. Quantity B is a number, or

2. Quantity B is an unknown value.

For both situations, the process is the same: Establish what you **need to know**.

3. Establish what you **know:**

    a. *Set up equations* to solve for previously unknown lines and angles, and

    b. *Make inferences* based on the properties of shapes.

4. Establish what you **don't know**:

    a. Take unknown values to extremes.

    b. If both quantities contain unknown values, look to gauge *relative size*.

And remember, no matter what, *don't trust the picture.*

Variable Creation

Take a look at another example of a Geometry Quantitative Comparison in which both quantities are unknown values:

Quantity A	**Quantity B**
v	*w*

As in the preceding example, there are no numbers given, so an exact value for any of these angles is impossible to determine. This does not, however, mean that the answer is necessarily (D).

What you **need to know** is the relative size of *v* and *w*. As this type of problem gets more difficult, it becomes more difficult to establish what you **know**. An important feature of this diagram is that the intersection of the three lines creates a triangle. Triangles, when they appear, are often very important parts of diagrams, because there are many rules related to triangles that test makers can make use of.

This question appears to be about angles. After all, the values in both quantities are angles. *Create variables* to represent the three angles of the triangle:

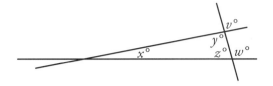

Part of the challenge is the fact that there are actually many relationships, and thus many equations you could create. For instance:

$$x + y + z = 180$$
$$w + z = 180$$

But not all of these relationships will help determine the relative size of v and w. You need to find relationships that will allow you to directly compare v and w.

The best bet for a link between v and w is the triangle in the center of the diagram. Try to express v and w in terms of x, y, and z.

Begin with v. Angles v and y are vertical angles, and thus equal. In Quantity A, replace v with y:

Quantity A	**Quantity B**
$v = y$	w

Now, if you can express w in terms of y, then you may be able to determine the relative size of v and w.

Based on the diagram, you know $w + z = 180$, so $w = 180 - z$.

Quantity A	**Quantity B**
y	$w = 180 - z$

You can't directly compare y and $(180 - z)$, so keep going. Try to find an equation that links y and z.

Remember, you also know that $x + y + z = 180$. Isolate z:

$$x + y + z = 180$$
$$z = 180 - x - y$$

Now, substitute $(180 - x - y)$ for z in Quantity B:

Quantity A	**Quantity B**
y	$180 - (180 - x - y) =$
	$x + y$

Now you can directly compare the two quantities. You know that x and y both represent angles, and so must be positive, so $x + y$ must be greater than y. The correct answer is **(B)**.

By the way, you've just proven that the exterior angle (w) is equal to the sum of the two remote interior angles ($x + y$). This is true in every case:

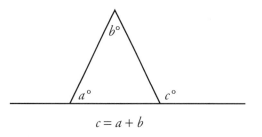

$$c = a + b$$

This is a good rule to know!

Strategy Tip: If a diagram presents a common shape, such as a triangle or a quadrilateral, it is often helpful to create variables to represent unknown angles or lengths. Once you've created variables, you can:

1. create equations, based on the properties of the shape
2. compare the relative size of both quantities using common variables

---

Word Geometry

This section is devoted to QC questions that test your knowledge of Geometry, but don't provide a picture. For example:

4 points, *P, Q, R,* and *T* lie in
a plane. *PQ* is parallel to *RT*
and *PR = QT*.

Quantity A	**Quantity B**
PQ	*RT*

The basic process remains the same. First, establish what you **need to know**.

Both quantities contain unknown values, so you need to determine the relative size of each line segment.

Now, establish what you **know**. For *any* Word Geometry question, the first thing you need to do is draw the picture.

You want to draw a picture that is accurate, but quick. And remember, you can always redraw the figure if you run into trouble.

For this question, the easiest way to start is to draw the parallel lines:

You know that points *P* & *Q* lie on one line, and *R* & *T* lie on the other, but you don't know their relative sizes. But you do know that *PR* = *QT*:

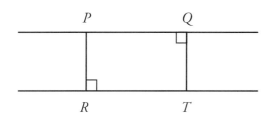

To start, the easiest thing to do is align the points so that they form a rectangle. Now, *PR* = *QT*. This diagram reflects all the information provided.

Now, take another look at the quantities:

<table>
<tr><td><u>**Quantity A**</u></td><td><u>**Quantity B**</u></td></tr>
<tr><td>*PQ*</td><td>*RT*</td></tr>
</table>

5

According to the diagram, *PQ* = *RT*.   A̶ B̶ C D

You're not done. You need to *try to prove* (D).

Now, the final step: establish what you **don't know**. Remember that the diagram above is only one possible way to represent the common information. Ask yourself, "What can change in this diagram?"

In the diagram above, *PQ* and *RT* were drawn perpendicular to the two parallel lines. But the angle can change. Redraw the diagram with *PR* and *QT* slanted:

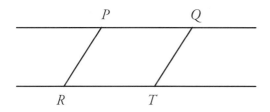

This diagram represents another possible configuration of the four points. Now how does *PQ* compare to *RT*?

Although it may not be immediately obvious, *PQ* is still equal to *RT*. Whereas the first diagram created a rectangle, this diagram has created a parallelogram. For additional practice, prove that *PQRT* is a parallelogram.

It may be tempting to choose choice (C) at this stage. But be careful! The key to Word Geometry questions is to avoid making *any* assumptions not explicitly stated in the common information.

It is not sufficient to merely change the diagram. Ask yourself, "What can I change in the diagram to change the relative size of *PQ* and *RT*?"

Changing the angle at which segments *PR* and *QT* intersected the parallel lines was not sufficient to achieve different results. What else can change?

The two diagrams above share a common feature that is not required by the common information: *PR* and *QT* are parallel.

Redraw the figure so that *PR* and *QT* are NOT parallel, but still equal:

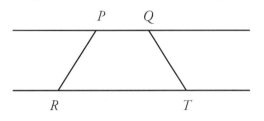

In this version of the diagram, *RT* is clearly longer than *PQ*. The answer is **(D)**.

Strategy Tip: Word Geometry problems follow the same basic process:

1. Establish what you **need to know**.
2. Establish what you **know**.
   a. Draw the picture.
   b. If you're trying to prove (D), you may need to redraw the picture.
3. Establish what you **don't know**.
   a. Ask yourself, "What changes to the picture would affect the *relative size* of the quantities?

Using Numbers

For many Word Geometry Quantitative Comparison questions, using numbers is an effective technique.

This technique is most effective when the question references specific dimensions of a shape (e.g., length, width, radius) but provides no actual numbers. For example:

Rectangles *R* and *S* have equal
areas. Rectangle *R*'s length is
greater than Rectangle *S*'s width.

Quantity A
The area of Rectangle *R* if
the length increases 30%

Quantity B
The area of Rectangle *S* if
the width increases 30%

First, establish what you **need to know**. Both quantities have an unknown value, so you will have to judge their relative size.

The best way to judge the relative size of each quantity is to use numbers.

The common information states that the rectangles have equal areas. An easy number to use for the area is 10. The numbers chosen in this example are only one set of possibilities, but they were chosen because they are easy to use:

$$\text{Area}_R = \text{Area}_S = 10$$

Now, draw the picture. Make sure you include the numbers you chose.

Each rectangle has an area of 10, but the length of R is greater than the width of S:

Quantity A mentions the length of R and Quantity B mentions the width of S. Pick values for the length and width of R and S.

Make the length of R 10 and the width 1. Make the length of S 2 and the width 5:

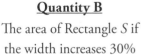

Quantity A

The area of Rectangle R if the length increases 30%

Quantity B

The area of Rectangle S if the width increases 30%

Now, evaluate the quantities. Start with Quantity A. Increase the length of *R* by 30%:

130% of 10 = (1.3)(10) = 13

The new area of *R* is $l \times w = (13)(1) = 13$:

Quantity A	**Quantity B**

R

13   1

13

The area of Rectangle *S* if the width increases 30%

Now, evaluate Quantity B. Increase the width of *S* by 30%:

130% of 5 = (1.3)(5) = 6.5

Use the calculator for this computation, if need be.

The new area of *S* is $l \times w = (2)(6.5) = 13$:

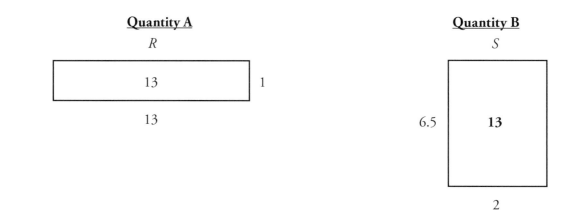

Quantity A

R

13   1

13

Quantity B

S

6.5   13

2

The new areas are equal. This result will hold regardless of the precise length you choose. The correct answer is **(C)**.

Strategy Tip: When a Word Geometry question references specific dimensions (e.g., length, width, radius) but does not provide actual numbers, Using numbers is a viable strategy.

To successfully use numbers, remember the following:

1. Pick numbers that match any restrictions in the common information or statements.

2. Try to prove (D) by testing several valid cases.

3. Look for patterns that suggest the answer is (A), (B), or (C).

Problem Set

1.

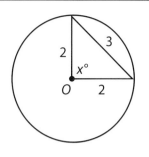

O is the center of the circle.

Quantity A	**Quantity B**
x	90

2.

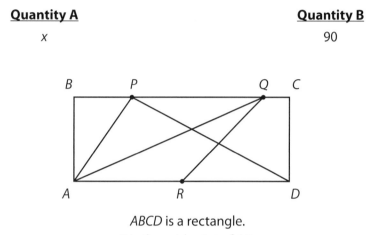

ABCD is a rectangle.
R is the midpoint of AD.

Quantity A	**Quantity B**
The area of Triangle APD	Twice the area of Triangle AQR

3.   The circumference of Circle A is twice the circumference of Circle B.

Quantity A	**Quantity B**
The area of Circle A	Twice the area of Circle B

4.   1,600 feet of fencing is used to enclose a square plot.

Quantity A	**Quantity B**
The plot's new area if the length were reduced by 4 feet and the width increased by 4 feet	The plot's new area if the length were equal to 398 feet and the width were equal to 402 feet

5.

Quantity A	**Quantity B**
The third side of an isosceles triangle with sides of 3 and 9	The third side of an isosceles triangle with sides of 6 and 8

6.

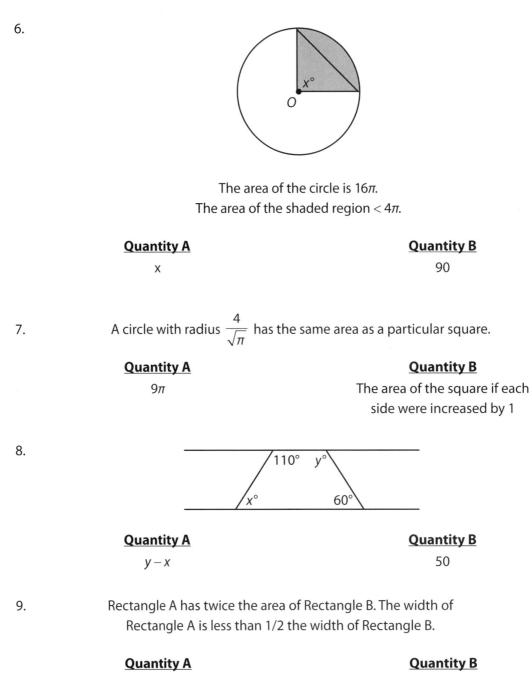

The area of the circle is 16π.
The area of the shaded region $< 4\pi$.

Quantity A	**Quantity B**
x	90

7.   A circle with radius $\dfrac{4}{\sqrt{\pi}}$ has the same area as a particular square.

Quantity A	**Quantity B**
9π	The area of the square if each side were increased by 1

8.

Quantity A	**Quantity B**
$y - x$	50

9.   Rectangle A has twice the area of Rectangle B. The width of Rectangle A is less than 1/2 the width of Rectangle B.

Quantity A	**Quantity B**
The area of Rectangle A	The area of Rectangle B if its width is increased by more than 2

10. l_1 and l_2 are parallel lines, and none of the lines in the figure are vertical.

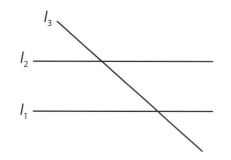

Quantity A   **Quantity B**

The slope of line l_1 minus   The slope of line l_2 minus
the slope of line l_3 the slope of line l_3

5

Answer Key

1. (A)   2. (C)   3. (A)   4. (B)   5. (A)   6. (B)   7. (A)   8. (D)   9. (D)   10. (C)

Solutions

1. **(A):** Use Quantity B as a benchmark by trying to make x equal to 90. That is, try to prove (C). If it doesn't work, you'll have your answer. Mark the angle as 90 and use the Pythagorean Theorem to find the hypotenuse, using the two legs of 2:

$$2^2 + 2^2 = (c)^2$$
$$c^2 = 8$$
$$c = \sqrt{8}$$
$$c = 2\sqrt{2} \approx 2(1.4) = 2.8$$

However, you know that the hypotenuse is actually 3, not 2.8. The bigger the hypotenuse, the larger angle x is going to be (picture how the triangle opens as x increases). If angle x were 90, the hypotenuse would be about 2.8. However, the hypotenuse is actually 3, so angle x must be greater than 90.

The answer is (A).

2. **(C):** There are no numbers mentioned anywhere in the problem, but that doesn't mean the answer is (D). Some important observations: both of the triangles mentioned in the quantities have the same height (that of the rectangle, which is AB). Also, since R is the midpoint of AD, the base of triangle APD is exactly twice the base of triangle AQR:

Quantity A	**Quantity B**
The area of triangle $APD =$	Twice the area of triangle $AQR =$
$\dfrac{1}{2}(AD)(AB)$	$2 \times \dfrac{1}{2}(AR)(AB) = (AR)(AB) =$
	$\dfrac{1}{2}(AD)(AB)$

You could use numbers to make the comparison easier. Note that if this is the only approach you take, you should try to prove (D) by testing several cases and confirming whether any emerging pattern makes sense. Let the height of each triangle (also the height of the rectangle) be 5. Let AD be 8, so $AR = RD = 4$:

Quantity A	**Quantity B**
The area of triangle $APD =$	Twice the area of triangle $AQR =$
$\dfrac{1}{2}(8)(5) = \mathbf{20}$	$2 \times \dfrac{1}{2}(4)(5) = \mathbf{20}$

Thus, the two quantities are equal. If you tried different numbers, you would continue to get this result, a pattern that makes sense based on the way identical numbers are input into both quantities.

Of course, you could also use variables here; for instance, let the height be x and DC and RC each be y. The quantities will each come out equal to xy.

The answer is (C).

3. **(A):** Since the formula for circumference is simply $C = 2\pi r$, doubling the radius will double the circumference (this is NOT true for the area formula, which involves *squaring* the radius). Thus, from the common information "The circumference of Circle A is twice the circumference of Circle B," you can infer that the radius of A is twice that of B.

For instance, say A's radius is 2 and B's radius is 1. In that case, the area of Circle A is 4π, so Quantity A = 4π. The area of Circle B is π, so Quantity B = 2π. Quantity A is greater.

This will work for any numbers you decide to use. If a circle's radius is double another circle's radius, its area will be four times as big, because the double-radius is then squared. The answer is (A).

4. **(B):** A square has a perimeter of 1,600 feet. To find the length of each side of the square, divide 1,600 by 4, because each side has the same length. The length of each side of the square is 400.

Quantity A asks you about a 396 by 404 rectangle, and Quantity B asks you about a 398 by 402 rectangle. Using the calculator, you get 396 × 404 = 159,984 for Quantity A and 398 × 402 = 159,996 for Quantity B.

The answer is (B).

Notice that if two numbers have a finite sum (396 + 404 = 800 and 398 + 402 = 800), their product will get larger as the two numbers get closer together. For example, 4 × 4 is greater than 3 × 5, 99 × 101 is greater than 97 × 103, and so on for any similar example you can think of.

In geometry, for a finite perimeter, the area of a shape is maximized by making the shape as regular as possible. That is, the more equilateral the shape, the greater the area. Thus, a square has greater area than any other rectangle with the same perimeter. The rectangle in Quantity B is closer to square than the rectangle in Quantity A, and thus it has the greater area.

5. **(A):** This is a question about the Third Side Rule, which says that the third side of a triangle must be less than the sum of the other two sides and greater than their difference. The triangle referenced in Quantity A has two sides of 3 and 9. By the Third Side Rule, the third side must be between 6 and 12 (the difference and the sum of 3 and 9). Since the triangle is isosceles and two sides must be of equal measure, the third side must be 9. (Also, try picturing a 3–3–9 triangle—it's impossible because the sides would never meet.)

The triangle referenced in Quantity B has two sides of 6 and 8. By the Third Side Rule, the third side must be between 2 and 14. Therefore, the third side could be either 6 or 8. Whether Quantity B is 6 or 8, it is definitely less than 9.

The answer is (A).

6. **(B):** Use Quantity B as a benchmark. If x were equal to 90, the shaded region would have an area equal to 1/4 that of the entire circle (since 90 is 1/4 of 360). Thus, if the angle were equal to 90, the shaded region would have an area of 4π (1/4 of the entire circle's area). Since the area of the shaded region is actually less than 4π, x must be less than 90.

The answer is (B).

7. **(A):** The radius of the circle is $\dfrac{4}{\sqrt{\pi}}$ and its area equals the area of the square. Plug $\dfrac{4}{\sqrt{\pi}}$ into the formula for area of a circle:

$$A = \pi \left(\frac{4}{\sqrt{\pi}} \right)^2$$
$$A = \pi \left(\frac{16}{\pi} \right)$$
$$A = 16$$

Thus, the area of the square is also 16 and the side is 4.

Quantity B is the area of the square if each side were increased by 1; that is, if each side were now equal to 5. Thus, Quantity B = 25. Quantity A is simply equal to 9π. Since π is more than 3, Quantity A is more than 27.

The answer is (A).

8. **(D):** Note that you are *not* told that the two horizontal-seeming lines in the figure are actually parallel, so you may *not* assume this. You do know that all four angles of the quadrilateral must sum to 360, so you can deduce that $x + y$ must equal 190.

However, without knowing that you have parallel lines, you have no way of knowing how to split up the 190 between x and y, and therefore no way of knowing whether $y - x$ is greater than 50. (For instance, if the lines were parallel, y would equal 120 and x would equal 70, and $y - x$ would be exactly 50. Adjust the figure even one degree—for instance, if y gets larger, x will get proportionately smaller—and $y - x$ will no longer equal 50.)

The answer is (D).

9. **(D):** Rectangle A has twice the area of Rectangle B and less than 1/2 the width. Start by drawing one scenario of how this could be:

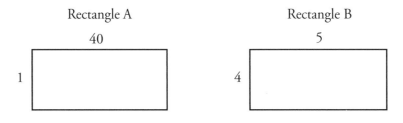

Rectangle A   Rectangle B

40   5

1   4

Now, try to prove D.

In this scenario, Quantity A equals 40.

In Quantity B, Rectangle B's width is increased by "more than 2." (Note that because you were not given any real numbers so far, it's likely that you could come up with a scenario in which this increase of "more than 2" yields a larger Quantity B and another scenario in which it does not—(D) should feel like a good guess to you here.)

Thus, Rectangle B now has a width of more than 6. Its area is now more than 30. But more than 30 could still be less than 40, or it could be more.

The answer is (D).

10. **(C):** This one's quick. This question is simply a test of the fact that parallel lines have equal slopes. Therefore, the slope of line l_1 and the slope of line l_2 are identical, and Quantities A and B are equal, regardless of the slope of line l_3.

The answer is (C).

Chapter 6 of

Quantitative Comparisons & Data Interpretation

Number Properties

In This Chapter...

Chapter 6

Number Properties

Number Properties turns out to be very fertile ground for Quantitative Comparison questions. By creating situations that hinge on the general behavior of negative numbers or of fractions raised to an exponent, ETS can create conceptually challenging problems that do not require a lot of calculation. A very popular theme related to Number Properties is *trying to prove* (D).

Positives & Negatives

Perhaps no dichotomy is as important to Quantitative Comparisons as is the Positive/Negative distinction. For one thing, ETS can easily create a question about positives and negatives without having to use either word. But there are common clues. If you see any of the following clues in a QC question, ask yourself whether positive and negative numbers play a role:

1. Common information states that a variable is either greater than or less than 0:

   $x < 0$ → x is negative

   $y > 0$ → y is positive

2. The product of more than one variable is greater than or less than 0:

   $pq > 0$ → p and q have the same sign; they are either both positive or both negative

3. An expression that contains both a negative sign and an exponent:

   $(-x)^4$ → $(-x)^4$ is positive, since 4 is even

Greater Than or Less Than 0

These clues often mean that you can save time by making generalizations based on the signs of variables. For example:

$$x < 0$$

Quantity A	**Quantity B**
$x - 2$	$-(x - 2)$

You want not only to get this question right, but to get it right *quickly*. One option is to plug in numbers for *x*.

For instance, plug in −1 for *x*:

$$x < 0$$

Quantity A	**Quantity B**
$(-1) - 2 = -3$	$-((-1) - 2) = 3$

When $x = -1$, Quantity B is bigger.   ̶A̶ B ̶C̶ D

But do you know Quantity B will *always* be bigger? No, you would need to try other numbers for *x*, and that will be time-consuming.

Instead, see whether you can make a generalization about the sign of each of the quantities. If *x* is negative, can you say anything definite about the sign of $x - 2$? Yes, you can. A negative minus a positive will always be negative.

You can rewrite Quantity A:

$$x < 0$$

Quantity A	**Quantity B**
Negative	$-(x - 2)$

Now you need to see whether you can make a generalization about Quantity B. Start with the expression inside the parentheses: $x - 2$. You know that $x - 2$ is always negative, so you can rewrite the expression as:

– (NEGATIVE)

What you have is a negative number inside the parentheses being multiplied by a negative:

$(x - 2)$ is negative, so $-(x - 2)$ is positive

You can rewrite Quantity B:

$$x < 0$$

Quantity A	**Quantity B**
Negative	Positive

Instead of trying specific numbers, you made generalizations about the sign of each quantity. *Any* positive number is greater than *any* negative number, so Quantity B will *always* be greater. The correct answer is (B).

Strategy Tip: If you are told the sign of a variable (e.g., $x < 0$), try to make a generalization about the sign of each quantity.

MANHATTAN
PREP

Product of Variables Greater Than or Less Than 0

In the last problem, you knew the sign of the variable. That will not always be the case:

$$xy > 0$$

Quantity A	**Quantity B**
$x + y$	0

This question is still about positives and negatives, but now it concerns the signs of both x and y. The common information is telling you something very important. There are two possible scenarios:

1. x and y are *both* positive.

2. x and y are *both* negative.

To find the answer, you need to test both scenarios. As in the last problem, you are testing *not* with specific numbers, but with the signs of the variables.

First, test the first scenario: x and y are both positive:

$$xy > 0$$

Quantity A	**Quantity B**
$x + y$	0
Positive + Positive =	
Positive	

If x and y are positive, Quantity A will always be positive, regardless of the values of x and y.   A B̸ ¢ D

Now, test the second scenario: x and y are both negative.

$$xy > 0$$

Quantity A	**Quantity B**
$x + y$	0
Negative + Negative =	
Negative	

If x and y are negative, Quantity A will always be negative, regardless of the values of x and y. The correct answer is **(D)**.

Strategy Tip: When the product of more than one variable is either greater than or less than 0, consider all possible signs and test all possible scenarios.

If $xy > 0$, the two scenarios are:

1. x and y are *both* positive.
2. x and y are *both* negative.

If $xy < 0$, the two scenarios are:

1. x is positive and y is negative.
2. x is negative and y is positive.

You will have to test *both* scenarios to get the right answer consistently.

Exponents & Negatives

Another sign that you are dealing with positives and negatives is the combination of exponents and negative signs:

n is an integer.

Quantity A	**Quantity B**
$(-3)^{2n}$	$(-3)^{2n+1}$

When negative numbers are raised to a power, they follow a pattern:

1. Negative numbers raised to odd powers are negative.
2. Negative numbers raised to even powers are positive.

You need to see if you can make a generalization about the sign of each quantity. Start with Quantity A: n is an integer, so $2n$ will always be even. The exponent will always be even, and a negative raised to an even power will always be positive:

n is an integer.

Quantity A	**Quantity B**
$(\text{Negative})^{\text{Even}} = \text{Positive}$	$(-3)^{2n+1}$

Now, test Quantity B: $2n$ is always even, which means $2n + 1$ will always be odd. A negative number raised to an odd power is negative:

n is an integer.

Quantity A	**Quantity B**
$(\text{Negative})^{\text{Even}} = \text{Positive}$	$(\text{Negative})^{\text{Odd}} = \text{Negative}$

The correct answer is **(A)**.

Strategy Tips: All of these problems have one thing in common: you can save time by figuring out whether each quantity is positive or negative.

Be on the lookout for these clues:

1. Common information states that a variable is greater than or less than 0 (e.g., $x > 0$, $p < 0$).

2. Common information states the product of two variables is greater than or less than 0 (e.g., $xy < 0$).

3. An expression contains both an exponent and a negative sign (e.g., $(-2)^x$).

When problems contain both exponents and negative signs, try to make generalizations about the sign of each quantity:

1. A negative number raised to an *odd* power is *negative*.

2. A negative number raised to an *even* power is *positive*.

Exponents

The test makers love the following exponent rules:

1. Numbers greater than 1 get *bigger* you raise them to higher powers:

$$2^1 < 2^2 < 2^3$$
$$2 < 4 < 8$$

2. Numbers between 0 and 1 get *smaller* as you raise them to higher powers:

$$\left(\frac{1}{2}\right)^1 > \left(\frac{1}{2}\right)^2 > \left(\frac{1}{2}\right)^3$$
$$\frac{1}{2} > \frac{1}{4} > \frac{1}{8}$$

When you see variables raised to exponents, don't forget about proper fractions (numbers between 0 and 1)!

Be on the lookout for questions that involve exponents and either fractions or variables that can be fractions:

x and *y* are positive.

Quantity A	**Quantity B**
xy	$(xy)^2$

At first, this question may seem to be about positives and negatives. But, if x and y are both positive, both quantities will be positive. You cannot make a quick comparison using positives and negatives.

The key to this question is the exponent. You have the same combination of variables raised to different powers:

x and *y* are positive.

Quantity A	**Quantity B**
$(xy)^1$	$(xy)^2$

First, try numbers greater than 1 for *x* and *y*. Plug in 2 for *x* and 3 for *y*:

x and *y* are positive.

Quantity A	**Quantity B**
$(2)(3) = \mathbf{6}$	$((2)(3))^2 = 6^2 = \mathbf{36}$

In this case, Quantity B is bigger.   A̶ B C̶ D

Don't stop there. You need to try to PROVE (D). The common information did not tell you that *x* and *y* are integers—you should see what happens if they are fractions.

Plug in $\dfrac{1}{2}$ for *x* and $\dfrac{1}{3}$ for *y*:

x and *y* are positive.

Quantity A	**Quantity B**
$\left(\dfrac{1}{2}\right)\left(\dfrac{1}{3}\right) = \dfrac{1}{6}$	$\left(\left(\dfrac{1}{2}\right)\left(\dfrac{1}{3}\right)\right)^2 = \left(\dfrac{1}{6}\right)^2 = \dfrac{1}{36}$

Fractions get smaller as they are raised to higher powers, so now Quantity A is larger than Quantity B. The correct answer is **(D)**.

Strategy Tip: On questions that involve variables and exponents, try to prove (D). Try numbers *greater than* 1 and numbers *between* 0 *and* 1.

1. Numbers greater than 1 get *bigger* as you raise them to higher powers
2. Numbers between 0 and 1 get *smaller* as you raise them to higher powers

---

Consecutive Integers

QC questions will sometimes ask you to compare the sum or product of sets of consecutive integers. The trick is to avoid finding the actual sums or products by *eliminating overlap*:

Quantity A

The product of all the integers from 2 to 23, inclusive

Quantity B

The product of all the integers from 5 to 24, inclusive

Both of these products are far too large to calculate in a reasonable amount of time, even with a calculator. Instead, you need to figure out which numbers appear in both products, and cancel those numbers.

In this problem, the numbers 5 through 23 appear in both sets. You can rewrite the products as:

Quantity A

$2 \times 3 \times 4 \times (5 \times 6 \times \ldots 22 \times 23)$

Quantity B

$(5 \times 6 \times \ldots 22 \times 23) \times 24$

The product of the numbers 5 through 23 is positive, and has the same value in each quantity. Therefore, because of the *invisible inequality*, you can divide out $(5 \times 6 \times \ldots 22 \times 23)$, and focus on what is left:

Quantity A

$$\frac{2 \times 3 \times 4 \times (5 \times 6 \times \ldots 22 \times 23)}{(5 \times 6 \times \ldots 22 \times 23)} =$$

$2 \times 3 \times 4 = 24$

Quantity B

$$\frac{(5 \times 6 \times \ldots 22 \times 23) \times 24}{(5 \times 6 \times \ldots 22 \times 23)} =$$

24

The values in the two quantities are equal. The correct answer is **(C)**.

Strategy Tip: To compare the sums or products of sets of consecutive integers, eliminate overlap in order to make a direct comparison.

Problem Set

1.   *x* is an integer.

Quantity A	**Quantity B**
$\dfrac{1}{100^x}$	$\dfrac{1}{99^x}$

2.   *n* is an integer.

Quantity A	**Quantity B**
$(-1)^{2n+1} \times (-1)^n$	$(1)^n$

3. $1 < 3x < 2$

Quantity A	**Quantity B**
x^5	x^7

4. $98 < x < 102$
                           $103 < y < 107$

Quantity A	**Quantity B**
$y - x$	$|y - x|$

5. $xyz < 0$

Quantity A	**Quantity B**
$x + y + z$	$2x + 2y + 2z$

6.

Quantity A	Quantity B
$(-101)^{102}$	$(-102)^{101}$

7.

$$n < -1$$

Quantity A	Quantity B
$n^2 \cdot n^4$	$(n^2)^4$

8.

Quantity A	Quantity B
The sum of the consecutive integers from −12 to 13	13

9.

$$\frac{x}{y} < 0$$
$$y > x$$

Quantity A	Quantity B
$y - x$	xy

10.

Quantity A	Quantity B
The sum of the consecutive integers from 2 to 15	34 less than the sum of the consecutive integers from 1 to 17

6

Answer Key

1. (D)   2. (D)   3. (A)   4. (C)   5. (D)   6. (A)   7. (B)   8. (C)   9. (A)   10. (C)

Solutions

1. **(D):** This question might be trying to trick you into picking (A) (the "greater looking" number) or maybe reasoning that a greater number under a fraction gets smaller, and therefore picking (B). But, of course, the exponent changes things. The easiest way to approach this is simply to plug in small values for x and try to prove (D). You know that x is an integer. Try some values for which it will be easy to calculate a value.

If $x = 1$, Quantity B is greater $\left(\dfrac{1}{99} > \dfrac{1}{100}\right)$.

If $x = 0$, the quantities are equal (since any number to a power of 0 is equal to 1).

Stop here—the answer is (D).

2. **(D):** Note that -1 and 1, when raised to an integer power, have very limited possibilities. -1 raised to an even power is 1, and -1 raised to an odd power is -1, whereas 1 raised to a power is always 1. Therefore, this is really a problem about odds and evens. So plug in a small even number and a small odd number and try to prove (D).

If $n = 2$, Quantity A is equal to $(-1)^5 \times (-1)^2$, which is -1, and Quantity B is equal to 1.

If $n = 3$, Quantity A is equal to $(-1)^7 \times (-1)^3$, which is 1, and Quantity B is equal to 1.

Stop here—the answer is (D).

3. **(A):** Before proceeding to Quantities A and B, simplify $1 < 3x < 2$ by dividing through by 3:

$$\frac{1}{3} < x < \frac{2}{3}$$

x is therefore between $\dfrac{1}{3}$ and $\dfrac{2}{3}$. More importantly, x is definitely between 0 and 1, which means it gets smaller when multiplied by itself.

Therefore, x^5 is larger than x^7.

The answer is (A).

(It would be possible to plug in a value between 1/3 and 2/3, such as 1/2, which would make Quantity A equal to $\dfrac{1}{32}$ and Quantity B equal to $\dfrac{1}{128}$. However, a Number Properties approach is far superior here—because you know that x will behave in a certain way due to its being a fraction between 0 and 1, you are saved from having to calculate anything to the 7th power).

6

4. **(C):** The presence of fairly large numbers in the common information is merely a distraction—the point is that y is definitely larger than x. Therefore, $y - x$ is positive. A positive number is the same as its own absolute value. Therefore, the answer is (C).

5. **(D):** Try to make generalizations about the signs of variables. If xyz is negative, then there are two possible scenarios: all three are negative, or one is negative and the other two are positive. To find the answer, you need to test both scenarios.

If all three are negative, then both Quantity A and Quantity B have negative values. Since you can factor the 2 out of Quantity B to get $2(x + y + z)$, Quantity B's value is therefore twice Quantity A's value—that is, Quantity B becomes *more negative* and is therefore smaller. Quantity A would be greater.

But if one of the variables were negative and the other two were positive, you wouldn't have enough information to know the sign of $x + y + z$ (remember, when multiplying or dividing, knowing the signs of what you are multiplying or dividing is enough to know the sign of the answer, but when adding or subtracting, you need to know the relative sizes of what you are adding or subtracting). For instance, if x, y, and z are -1, 3, and 4, then $x + y + z$ is positive, and $2x + 2y + 2z$ (Quantity B) would be greater.

The answer is (D).

6. **(A):** A good sign that a problem can perhaps be solved with just positives and negatives is the presence of both exponents and negative signs. Using only positives and negatives, consider the problem as such:

Quantity A	**Quantity B**
$(\text{Negative})^{\text{even}}$	$(\text{Negative})^{\text{odd}}$

Thus, Quantity A is positive and Quantity B is negative.

The answer is (A).

7. **(B):** Use exponent rules to simplify the expressions in each quantity:

Quantity A	**Quantity B**
$n^2 \times n^4 = n^6$	$(n^2)^4 = n^8$

In both quantities, n is raised to an even power, so both quantities will be positive. Because $n < -1$, the absolute value of n will get bigger as n is raised to higher powers. Therefore, Quantity B will be greater.

8. **(C):** If you were to write out the integers in Quantity A, you'd have $-12 + -11 + -10 \ldots + -1 + 0 + 1 \ldots + 10 + 11 + 12 + 13$.

Note that for every negative there is a corresponding positive value. For instance, -12 cancels with 12, -11 cancels with 11, and so on. When all the canceling is through, you're left with 13.

The answer is (C).

9. **(A):** The common information is enough for you to know that this is a Positive/Negative question. If x/y is negative, then x and y have different signs. If $y > x$, then y must be positive and x negative. In Quantity A, you have a positive minus a negative—this will create a greater positive. In Quantity B, you have a negative times a positive, which is always negative.

The answer is (A).

10. **(C):** To compare the sums or products of sets of consecutive integers, eliminate overlap in order to make a direct comparison. You can abbreviate "the sum of the consecutive integers from 2 to 15" as $(2 + 3 \ldots + 15)$:

Quantity A	**Quantity B**
$(2 + 3 \ldots + 15)$	$1 + (2 + 3 \ldots + 15) + 16 +$ $17 - 34$

Now, eliminate $(2 + 3 \ldots + 15)$ from both sides:

Quantity A	**Quantity B**
0	$1 + 16 + 17 - 34$

Since $1 + 16 + 17 - 34 = 0$, the answer is (C).

6

Chapter 7

of

Quantitative Comparisons
& Data Interpretation

Word Problems

In This Chapter...

Ratios

Statistics

Chapter 7

Word Problems

Word Problems (WPs) very much fit into the framework of avoiding excessive computation. Difficult WP questions are often difficult because they describe situations that do not translate obviously into solvable equations.

But there is an added wrinkle: WP questions do not automatically provide enough information to solve for the desired values. For example:

Milo can core x apples in 10 minutes
and peel y potatoes in 20 minutes.

Quantity A	Quantity B
The number of apples Milo can core in an hour	The number of potatoes Milo can peel in an hour

The rate at which Milo can core apples is x apples/10 min, or $6x$ apples/hour. The rate at which Milo can peel potatoes is y potatoes/20 min, or $3y$ potatoes/hour. So the comparison is really $6x$ vs. $3y$. But without more information, you have no way to compare these two values. The answer is **(D)**.

Strategy Tip: Whenever you see a word problem on Quantitative Comparisons, make sure you have the information you need before doing any computation. If you don't have enough info, the answer is (D).

Ratios

Don't confuse a ratio with actual numbers of objects. For instance, if you know that a store carries red shirts and white shirts in a 2 to 3 ratio, the store may have 5 total shirts (2 red and 3 white), 10 total shirts (4 red and 6 white), 500 total shirts (200 red and 300 white), etc. What you do know is that there are more reds than whites and that the total number of shirts must be a multiple of 5.

Adding real numbers of objects to a ratio isn't very helpful without some real numbers of objects to begin with. For example, if a store carries red shirts and white shirts in a 2 to 3 ratio, what effect does adding 3 red shirts have? Well, if the store had 5 total shirts (2 red and 3 white), adding 3 red shirts changes the ratio to 5 to 3 (5 red and 3 white). But if you started with 500 total shirts (200 red and 300 white), adding 3 red shirts doesn't change the ratio very much at all; it's now 203 to 300. Try an example:

A university contains French majors and Spanish majors
in a 5 to 7 ratio.

Quantity A	**Quantity B**
The number of French majors if 10 French majors transfer into the university and no other students leave, join, or change majors	The number of French majors if 3/7 of the Spanish majors switch to French

Try to prove (D). Start by constructing two scenarios for "A university contains French majors and Spanish majors in a 5 to 7 ratio." For the first scenario, use the smallest possible values: 5 French majors and 7 Spanish majors. For the second scenario, use much larger (but still easy to work with) numbers: 500 French majors and 700 Spanish majors.

Evaluate the first scenario. For the first scenario (5 French majors and 7 Spanish majors), Quantity A gives us 15 French majors (5 + 10 = 15). In Quantity B, 3 Spanish majors switch to French $\left(\frac{3}{7} \times 7 = 3\right)$, so there are 8 French majors (5 + 3 = 8). In this scenario, Quantity A is greater.

Now, evaluate the second scenario (500 French majors and 700 Spanish majors). Quantity A gives you 510 French majors (500 + 10 = 510). In Quantity B, 300 Spanish majors switch to French $\left(\frac{3}{7} \times 700 = 300\right)$, so there are 800 total French majors. In this scenario, Quantity B is greater. The correct answer is **(D)**.

Strategy Tip: Remember that ratios provide NO information about actual values. To try to prove (D) on a ratios problem, choose one scenario in which the actual values are the same values as the ratio and choose another scenario in which the numbers are much larger (but still pick numbers that are easy to work with).

Statistics

Aside from the standard average formula (which you should know *very* well), there is another property of averages that is often tested in the Quantitative Comparison format. Try an example:

A company has two divisions. Division A has 105 employees and an average salary of $60,000. Division B has 93 employees and an average salary of $70,000.

Quantity A	**Quantity B**
The average salary of all the employees at the company	$65,000

A lot of unnecessary computation could go into answering this QC question. Notice that your benchmark value in Quantity B is exactly halfway between the average salaries of the two divisions. This is very convenient because you can use the principle of weighted averages.

Suppose that instead of 198 employees (105 + 93), you have 6 employees: 3 people in each division. To simplify things, you can say that everyone in Division A makes $60,000 and everyone in Division B makes $70,000.

The average salary for all 6 employees will be:

$$\frac{3(60,000) + 3(70,000)}{6} = 65,000$$

There are an equal number of people in each division, so the average salary is the average of 60,000 and 70,000.

Think of average salaries as a spectrum. There are three scenarios:

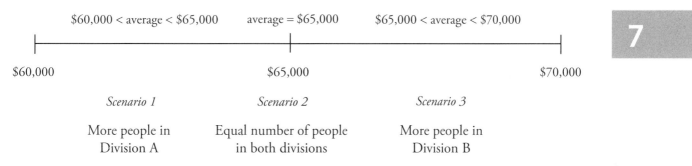

Scenario 1	*Scenario 2*	*Scenario 3*
More people in Division A	Equal number of people in both divisions	More people in Division B

The common information tells you there are more employees in Division A (105 vs. 93). The average salary of the whole company will be less than $65,000:

Quantity A	Quantity B
The average salary of all the employees at the company = **less than $65,000**	$65,000

The correct answer is (B).

Strategy Tip: In any question that involves two groups that have some kind of average value, use the principles of weighted averages.

If two groups have an equal number of members, the total average will be the average of the two groups

(e.g., $\dfrac{3(60,000)+3(70,000)}{6} = 65,000$).

If one group has more members, the total average will be closer to the average of that group

(e.g., $\dfrac{105(60,000)+93(70,000)}{198} = 64,696.97$). There's no need to do this calculation!

Problem Set

1.   Bag A contains red and black marbles in a 3 to 4 ratio.
                Bag B contains red and black marbles in a 4 to 3 ratio.

Quantity A	**Quantity B**
The total number of red marbles in both bags combined	The total number of black marbles in both bags combined

2.   June can run 6 laps in *x* minutes.
                 Miriam can run 11 laps in 2*x* minutes.

Quantity A	**Quantity B**
The number of minutes it takes June to run 24 laps	The number of minutes it takes Miriam to run 22 laps

3.   Abe's quiz scores are 62, 68, 74, and 68.
                Ben's quiz scores are 66 and 70.

Quantity A	**Quantity B**
The score Abe needs on his fifth quiz to raise his average to 70	The score Ben needs on his third quiz to raise his average to 70

4.   Set S = {2, 3, 5, 2, 11, 1}

Quantity A	**Quantity B**
The average of Set S	The mode of Set S if every number in the set were doubled

7

5.   Silky Dark Chocolate is 80% cocoa.
                Rich Milk Chocolate is 50% cocoa.
                Smooth White Chocolate is 0% cocoa.

Quantity A	**Quantity B**
Percent cocoa of a mixture of 3 parts Silky Dark Chocolate and 1 part Smooth White Chocolate	Percent cocoa of a mixture of 2 parts Rich Milk Chocolate and 1 part Silky Dark Chocolate

6.   The average of six numbers is 44.
                  The average of two of those numbers is 11.

Quantity A	**Quantity B**
The average of the other 4 numbers	77

7.   Tavi drives 113 miles at 50 miles per hour and returns
                    via the same route at 60 miles per hour.

Quantity A	**Quantity B**
Tavi's average speed for the entire round trip	55 mph

8.   Joe reaches into a bag containing 5 red, 4 blue, and 8 orange jellybeans,
                     and randomly selects three jellybeans.

Quantity A	**Quantity B**
The probability of selecting a red, then a blue, then an orange jellybean	The probability of selecting a red, then another red, then an orange jellybean

9.   Preeti can make 100 sandwiches in 1 hour and 15 minutes.
                   Mariska can make 50 sandwiches in 30 minutes.

Quantity A	**Quantity B**
The time it would take Preeti and Mariska to make a total of 180 sandwiches, each working at her own independent rate	The time it would take to make 110 sandwiches if Mariska worked alone for 30 minutes and then Mariska and Preeti worked together to finish the job

10.   A particular train travels from Town A to Town B at x miles per hour,
                  and then from Town B to Town C at $1.2x$ miles per hour.

Quantity A	**Quantity B**
The train's travel time from Town A to Town B	The train's travel time from Town B to Town C

MANHATTAN
PREP

Answer Key

1. (D)   2. (C)   3. (A)   4. (C)   5. (C)   6. (B)   7. (B)   8. (C)   9. (A)   10. (D)

Solutions

1. **(D):** While you have the red-to-black ratios for each of the two bags, you don't have any real numbers of marbles anywhere, so it's impossible to combine the two ratios. Here, you can try to prove (D). For instance, say each bag contains 7 marbles. In such a case, Bag A would have 3 red and 4 black, and Bag B would have 3 black and 4 red. Quantity A and Quantity B would then each be equal to 7.

However, what if Bag A contains 7 marbles and Bag B contains 700 marbles? Then Bag A would have 3 red and 4 black, and Bag B would have 400 red and 300 black. In such a case, Quantity A would be equal to 403 and Quantity B would be equal to 304.

The answer is (D).

2. **(C):** First, determine whether there's a shortcut here. June can run 6 laps in x minutes. If Miriam were equally fast, she could run 12 laps in $2x$ minutes (twice the laps in twice the time). As it turns out, Miriam can only do 11 laps in that time, so Miriam is slightly slower than June. If the quantities then asked for June and Miriam's times to run *the same number of laps,* you would not have to do any calculating: June is faster, so Miriam's time would be greater. However, June (the slightly faster person) is being asked to run slightly more laps, so it's pretty hard to estimate. Instead, use Rate × Time = Distance.

Since Rate × Time = Distance, Rate is equal to $\dfrac{\text{Distance}}{\text{Time}}$. Thus:

June's rate is $\dfrac{6}{x}$

Miriam's rate is $\dfrac{11}{2x}$

Quantity A asks for June's time to run 24 laps. Since Rate × Time = Distance, Time is equal to $\dfrac{\text{Distance}}{\text{Rate}}$. Therefore:

$$T = \dfrac{24}{\dfrac{6}{x}}$$

$$T = 24 \times \dfrac{x}{6}$$

$$T = 4x$$

June's time is $4x$.

Quantity B asks for Miriam's time to run 22 laps. Given that Time is equal to Distance/Rate:

$$T = \frac{22}{\frac{11}{2x}}$$

$$T = 22 \times \frac{2x}{11}$$

$$T = 4x$$

Miriam's time is also $4x$.

The answer is (C).

3. **(A):** This is an excellent example of a Word Problems problem for which no real calculation is needed if the idea of weighted averages is understood. Abe's current average is 68 (for a quick average, note that two scores *are* 68, and of the other two scores, one is six points over 68 and one is six points under 68, keeping the overall average at 68). Ben's average is also 68 (halfway between 66 and 70).

For Abe to get a 70 overall, his fifth score will have to compensate for four too-low scores. For Ben to get a 70 overall, his third score will only have to compensate for two too-low scores. So Abe will need a higher score to raise his average to 70 than Ben will. (This is the same as the more bad grades you have, the higher you have to get on the next quiz to pull your average back up.)

Actually doing this problem mathematically would take too much time, but for the curious, Abe's fifth score could be calculated as such:

$$\frac{62 + 68 + 74 + 68 + x}{5} = 70$$

As it turns out, Abe needs a 78.

Ben's third score could be calculated as such:

$$\frac{66 + 70 + x}{3} = 70$$

Ben needs a 74.

The answer is (A).

4. **(C):** There's no shortcut to find the average here. Simply add $2 + 3 + 5 + 2 + 11 + 1$ to get 24 and divide by 6 to get 4. Quantity A is therefore equal to 4.

Finding the mode is much easier (the mode is simply the number that occurs most often in the list). The current mode is 2. When you double everything in the list, the mode will then be 4. (The other numbers in the list are irrelevant—don't bother to double them).

The answer is (C).

5. **(C):** In Quantity A, you need the percent cocoa of a mix that is 3 parts dark and 1 part smooth white. So you will need to create a weighted average (that is, you need to count the dark chocolate three times in the average, since there's three times as much of it):

$$\frac{80 + 80 + 80 + 0}{4} = 60$$

Quantity A's mix will be 60% cocoa. Create a similar weighted average for Quantity B (2 parts milk, 1 part dark):

$$\frac{50 + 50 + 80}{3} = 60$$

Quantity B's mix will also be 60% cocoa.

The answer is (C).

6. **(B):** No actual calculation is required here. Six numbers average to 44 and two of them average to 11. That is, two of the numbers have an average that is 33 points below the overall average. Therefore, the other four numbers must bring the average up 33 points. However, since there are *four* numbers bringing the average up (versus *two* bringing the average down), each of the individual numbers doesn't have to "compensate" as much—they will not have to be as high as 77, which is 33 points above 44.

Put another way, since there are only two numbers dragging the average down, they have to be pretty extreme. But since there are four numbers dragging the average up, they get to share the burden—they don't have to be as extreme.

The answer is (B).

If you can master that logic, you can solve problems like this one very fast. However, if you prefer a more mathematical approach:

If six numbers average to 44, their sum is $6 \times 44 = 264$.
If two of the numbers average to 11, their sum is $2 \times 11 = 22$.
Thus, the other four numbers must sum to $264 - 22 = 242$.
$242/4 = 60.5$

Thus, the average of the other four numbers is 60.5, well under 77.

The answer is (B).

7. **(B):** No actual calculation is required here if you have a good grasp of average speed. First, Tavi's average speed is *not* 55 miles per hour—you cannot simply average the two speeds. Why? Because average speed is essentially what you would get if you clocked Tavi's speed during every second of the journey and then averaged all the seconds. If you wrote out a long, long list of all the numbers you'd be averaging, you'd have written out a lot more 50's than 60's, because Tavi spent more time driving at the slower speed. Therefore, Tavi's average speed will be "between 50 and 60 but closer to 50." (Note: this only works when the distances are *the same*). Therefore, 55 is higher than Tavi's average speed.

The answer is (B).

8. **(C):** Set up the probabilities in both quantities before calculating either value. The bag contains 5 red, 4 blue, and 8 orange jellybeans, and thus 17 total jellybeans.

In Quantity A, the probability of picking a red is $\dfrac{5}{17}$. Keep in mind that once the red is selected, there are only 16 jellybeans left in the bag, so the probability of then picking a blue is $\dfrac{4}{16}$, and then the probability of picking an orange is $\dfrac{8}{15}$. Thus, Quantity A is equal to $\dfrac{5}{17} \times \dfrac{4}{16} \times \dfrac{8}{15}$.

In Quantity B, the probability of picking a red first is, of course, still $\dfrac{5}{17}$. Notice that *once a red is picked first, there are now equal numbers of blues and reds left in the bag* (4 each). Thus, the probability of now picking another red is $\dfrac{4}{16}$ (equal to the probability in Quantity A of picking a blue at this point), and then the probability of picking an orange is still $\dfrac{8}{15}$. Thus, Quantity B is also equal to $\dfrac{5}{17} \times \dfrac{4}{16} \times \dfrac{8}{15}$.

The answer is (C).

You may have been tempted to multiply the fractions, but in this case no computation is necessary.

9. **(A):** To get started on a work problem, you need to convert Preeti and Mariska's sandwich speeds into rate format—that is, you need their information in a per hour format. If Preeti can make 100 sandwiches in 1 hour 15 minutes, that's 100 sandwiches in 75 minutes:

$$\frac{100 \text{ sandwiches}}{75 \text{ minutes}} = \frac{x \text{ sandwiches}}{60 \text{ minutes}}$$

$$6{,}000 = 75x$$
$$x = 80$$

Therefore, Preeti can make 80 sandwiches per hour.

Mariska's rate is much easier—if she can make 50 sandwiches in 30 minutes, just double the rate to get that she can make 100 sandwiches in 1 hour.

Now that the rates are in per hour format, you can add: 80 sandwiches/hour + 100 sandwiches/hour is a combined rate of 180 sandwiches/hour.

Fortunately, Quantity A asks for their time to make 180 sandwiches working together, so Quantity A is simply equal to 1 hour.

Quantity B asks for the time it would take to make 110 sandwiches if Mariska worked alone for 30 minutes and then the women finished the job together. Working alone for 30 minutes, Mariska will make 50 sandwiches. That leaves 60 sandwiches left for the two of them to make together:

$$\frac{180 \text{ standwiches}}{60 \text{ minutes}} = \frac{60 \text{ standwiches}}{x \text{ minutes}}$$

$$180x = 3600$$
$$x = 20$$

Or try this mental math shortcut: since the women working together can make 180 sandwiches/hour, it will take $\frac{1}{3}$ of the time to make $\frac{1}{3}$ of the sandwiches, so it will take $\frac{1}{3}$ of an hour, or 20 minutes. Either way, Quantity B is equal to the 30 minutes Mariska works alone, plus the 20 minutes it takes the women to finish the job together. Thus, Quantity B is equal to 50 minutes.

The answer is (A).

10. **(D):** As a reminder: whenever you see a Word Problem on Quantitative Comparisons, *make sure you have the information you need before doing any computation.*

Quantities A and B ask about travel time. From Rate × Time = Distance, you need both distance and rate in order to compute time. The common information gives you only two relative rates (x and $1.2x$). Without some information about the distances from A to B and B to C, there is no way to compute even a relative time.

The answer is (D).

7

Chapter 8

of

Quantitative Comparisons & Data Interpretation

Data Interpretation

In This Chapter...

The Basic Process of Solving a Data Interpretation Question

Data Interpretation Graphs and Charts–aka–The Graph Zoo

Chapter 8

Data Interpretation

Data Interpretation (DI) questions appear as sets of problems that refer to the same group of one to three related graphs or charts. On the revised GRE, you will see an average of two DI sets per exam, each with two or three associated problems.

DI questions are not, in general, particularly difficult. However, they can take a lot of time to solve if you aren't careful. It is very important to learn how to tackle them efficiently, using the on-screen calculator when appropriate.

The Basic Process of Solving a Data Interpretation Question

1. Scan the graph(s). (15–20 seconds)

- What type of graph is it?
- Is the data displayed in percentages or absolute quantities?
- Does the graph provide any overall total value?

2. Figure out what the question is asking. What does it ask you to do?

- Calculate a value?
- Establish how many data points meet a criterion?

3. Find the graph(s) with the needed information.

- Look for key words in the question.

4. *If* you need to establish how many data points meet a criterion, keep track as you go by taking notes.

5. *If* you need to perform a computation, translate the question into a mathematical expression *before* you try to solve it.

6. *If* one of the answer choices is "cannot be determined," check that you have *all* the information you need before performing any calculations.

7. Use the calculator when needed, but keep your eye out for opportunities to use time-saving estimation techniques:

- Does the question use the word "approximate"?
- Are the numbers in the answer choices sufficiently far apart?

This list of steps should be used as a high-level process checklist, to help you remember what to look for and do as you solve, but some of the steps are only relevant to some of the problems. The examples on the subsequent pages follow this process and show how to apply it to various types of problems.

Data Interpretation Graphs and Charts—aka—The Graph Zoo

Most GRE Data Interpretation questions focus on data in five standard formats. You will be much faster at extracting the data if you are already familiar with reading these types of tables and graphs. GRE DI charts always tell a data story, and the questions you will be answering are about that story. In order to understand these charts and how they work, you will be looking at a simple data story about a produce stand. The owner of the produce stand has some numbers for the amounts of the different types of produce sold per month over a one-year period. For one month, the owner also has some detailed data on exactly which fruits and vegetables were sold. How might the GRE present this story? There are various ways, but all involve the five basic types of charts.

As you work through the examples, you will notice that many problems also involve FDP calculations, and you will find that you will be much faster at those calculations if you already know various standard formulas, such as the percentage increase/decrease formula, and computation shortcuts, such as estimating fractions. You will also notice that the solutions to the problems point out the various computation tricks. Use the calculator when it's easy to, but also work on developing estimation techniques. This will ultimately save you time.

Look carefully at the solutions and you will also see that they follow the previously described problem-solving process. As an exercise, you might want to cover up the solution steps with a piece of paper and see if you can predict, from the general problem-solving process, what the next step should be as you work through the solution and uncover each step. Although there are many ways to solve these problems, time is critical on the GRE, and learning to follow a standard process and use computation shortcuts will ultimately save you a great deal of time and stress.

8

Pie Charts

A pie chart is used to show the relative sizes of slices as proportions of a whole. The size of the angle of the pie slice is proportional to the percentage of the whole for each item. Even if a pie chart shows amounts instead of percentages, data is shown in pies because percentages, or relative quantities, are important to the story. If you see data in a pie chart on the GRE, you know that there will be one or more questions about percentages or proportions.

Also, many pie charts include a total amount annotated on the chart. If you see this feature, you can be almost certain that the GRE will ask you to calculate an absolute quantity of some item shown in the pie and that the best way to do so will be to use that number and multiply it by the relevant percentage.

A pie chart can only show one series of data, so if you see two pies, which sometimes occurs on the GRE, they represent two series of data and you can be just about certain that one or more of the questions will ask you to compare something in the two different data series.

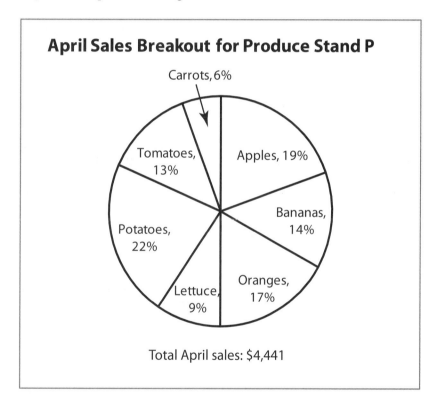

Below are some common calculations that you might be asked to perform on the example pie chart above, which shows the April sales breakout for the produce stand:

- Tomato sales = 13% of $4,441 = 0.13 × 4,441
- Lettuce & tomato sales = 9% of $4,441 + 13% of $4,441 = 22% of $4,441 = 0.22 × 4,441

1. Approximately what amount of total sales in April came from sales of apples, bananas, and oranges?

   (A) $2,221   (B) $2,362   (C) $2,495   (D) $2,571   (E) $2,683

The question asks for the sum of the absolute dollar amount of total sales of apples, bananas, and oranges.

The only chart you have is a pie chart showing percentages, so this question is asking you to convert from percents to dollar amounts.

You have apples at 19%, bananas at 14%, and oranges at 17%, and total sales were $4,441. So you need to set up a mathematical expression for the amount of sales that come from apples, bananas, and oranges:

$$(0.19 \times 4,441) + (0.14 \times 4,441) + (0.17 \times 4,441) = 2,220.5$$

You can do this more efficiently by summing the percentages before you multiply by the total sales:

$= 4,441 \times (0.19 + 0.14 + 0.17)$
$= 4,441 \times (0.50)$ Sum the percentage so you only multiply by one number.
$= 2,220.5$ The question says approximate, so A must be the answer.

2. If sales of potatoes were to increase by $173 next month and sales of all other items were held constant, approximately what percentage of the total sales would be potatoes?

   (A) 20%   (B) 25%   (C) 30%   (D) 35%   (E) 40%

The question asks the new ratio of potato sales to total sales, after adding $173 in potato sales.

The only chart you have is a pie chart showing percentages, but it has a total quantity and a percentage from potatoes: 22% of total sales are from potato sales and there is $4,441 in total sales.

Set up a mathematical expression:

$$\frac{0.22(4,441)+173}{4,441+173} = 0.249 \approx 25\%$$

Important: Note that the denominator of the fraction above takes into account that the $173 of new potato sales must be added not only to the potato sales but to the total sales as well. That is, the total sales is no longer the $4,441 from the chart, since additional sales have been made.

The answer is (B).

8

3. If the areas of the sectors in the circle graph are drawn in proportion to the percentages shown, what is the approximate measure, in degrees, of the sector representing the percent of total sales due to lettuce?

(A) 24 degrees   (B) 28 degrees   (C) 32 degrees   (D) 36 degrees   (E) 40 degrees

The question asks for the degree measure of the lettuce wedge on the chart.

The only chart you have is a pie chart showing percentages; that's the chart you use.

You have 9% of total sales from lettuce, so lettuce represents 9% of the 360-degree circle.

Writing this in math form, you get:

$0.09 \times 360 = 32.4$ degrees

The answer is (C).

Column Charts

A column chart shows amounts as heights. Typically, the *x*-axis is time (e.g., months, years) and column charts are used to show trends over time.

Often the hardest thing about a column chart is just reading the values. The GRE never makes an exact value reading critical to answering a question unless numeric values are explicitly given (and even then you can usually just round), so just raise your index finger up near the computer monitor, draw an imaginary line across the chart, and estimate approximate quantities.

Single Series Column Charts

A single data series chart is so straightforward that it doesn't usually even have a legend. Here is an example showing the produce stand's sales:

Some common calculations that you might be asked to perform are percentage increase or decrease from one time period to the next, or even more simply, just counting the number of periods when data values were above or below a particular value:

Approximate percentage increase in sales from April to May:

$$\frac{\text{May sales } - \text{April sales}}{\text{April sales}} \approx \frac{5,000 - 4,500}{4,500} = \frac{500}{4,500} \approx 11\%$$

Number of months when sales were less than February sales is 1.

1. In how many of the months shown were total produce sales greater than $4,600?

(A) 7   (B) 8   (C) 9   (D) 10   (E) 11

The question asks you to count the number of months shown that were greater than $4,600.

The only chart you have is this column chart, and it shows the sales for each month directly, so you can just read the chart.

Since most months appear to have sales greater than $4,600, count the number of months in which sales were less than $4,600 and subtract from the total number of months shown, which is 12.

Months when sales were less than $4,600: Jan, Feb, Mar, Apr, so number of months when sales were greater than $4,600 equals 12 − 4, or 8, and the answer is **(B)**.

> **Strategy Tip:** Use a piece of paper or even your finger to make a straight edge from halfway between the $4,000 and the $5,000 to make reading the graph easier.

Stacked Column Charts

The GRE is especially fond of stacked column charts because they can be used to show two or more data series at a time, as differently shaded parts of one column. For instance, "vegetable sales" and "fruit sales" sum to "total sales." This makes it as easy to answer questions that ask about the total as it is with just a single data series in the chart.

However, it is a little harder to read off vegetable sales by itself—you have to calculate total sales minus fruit sales, so you can be almost certain that you will have a question that asks you to do something like this.

Notice also in the example below, which breaks out the monthly sales of the produce stand into fruit and vegetable sales, that charts that show multiple data series have legends so you can tell which part of the bar represents which category:

2. Approximately what were total vegetable sales in September?

(A) $5,000   (B) $4,000   (C) $3,000   (D) $2,500   (E) $2,000

The question asks you to figure out vegetable sales in September.

The only chart you have is this column chart, and it shows the vegetable sales for each month directly, so you can just read the chart.

To get vegetable sales, you need total sales minus fruit sales. For September, that is equal to about $5,000 − $2,500, or $2,500 and the answer is (**D**).

Strategy Tip: Subtract in order to calculate many of the values shown in stacked bar graphs.

Clustered Column Charts

Another variation on column charts has clustered columns instead of stacked columns. Clustered column charts make it easier to compare the parts of the total, but more difficult to determine the actual total because you have to sum the columns.

The types of questions that would be asked about a clustered column chart are the same as those that would be asked about a stacked column chart. The only difference between the two types is that it is easier to read a total quantity off of a stacked column chart, but easier to read the height of an individual series item, such as total vegetable sales in June, off of a clustered column chart. The example below shows exactly the same data as the previous stacked column chart showed, except in the clustered column format:

3. Which month had the largest percentage of vegetable sales relative to total sales?

(A) Jan   (B) Mar   (C) Jun   (D) Oct   (E) Nov

The question asks you to compare the ratio of vegetable sales to total sales for several months.

The only chart you have is this column chart, and it shows the sales for each month directly, so you can just read the numbers and calculate the ratios.

The formula for the ratio of vegetable sales to total sales is:

$$\frac{\text{vegetable sales}}{\text{fruit sales} + \text{vegetable sales}}$$

The key to solving this problem is realizing that you don't have to do calculations for all of the months. In January and March, vegetable sales were substantially larger than fruit sales, so they were more than half of total sales, whereas in June, October, and November, they were about the same or actually less than fruit sales, so the only months you really have to look at are January and March.

8

Since the difference in fruit and vegetable sales is about the same in both months, but total sales are much greater in March, the same absolute difference in fruit sales is a greater percentage of the total sales in January than it is in March, so the answer is **(A)**.

You can verify this with a calculator:

$$\frac{\text{Jan vegetable sales}}{\text{Jan vegetable sales} + \text{Jan fruit sales}} \approx \frac{2,200}{1,700 + 2,200} = \frac{2,200}{3,900} \approx 0.56$$

$$\frac{\text{Mar vegetable sales}}{\text{Mar vegetable sales} + \text{Mar fruit sales}} \approx \frac{2,400}{2,000 + 2,400} = \frac{2,400}{4,400} \approx 0.55$$

Strategy Tip: Any given amount is a greater percentage of a smaller number than it is of a larger number.

Percentage Column Charts

Occasionally the GRE uses column charts to show percentages directly, rather than absolute quantities. If you see this type of chart, and you need quantity information, you will need another chart to provide actual values.

Otherwise, the types of questions that would be asked about a percentage column chart are the same as those that would be asked about a stacked column chart. The example below shows a typical percentage column chart:

4. If the total produce sales in July at Produce Stand P were $4,500, what were the approximate total fruit sales in December at Produce Stand P?

    (A) $2,100   (B) $2,200   (C) $2,300   (D) $2,400   (E) Cannot be determined

The question asks you to determine the amount of fruit sales in December.

The only chart you have is this column chart, and it shows the percentage of sales due to fruit and the percentage of sales due to vegetables for each month.

The formula for the amount of fruit sales in December is:

$$\text{Total fruit sales in December} = \%\ \text{fruit sales} \times \text{Total sales in December}$$

However, you have no information on total sales in December! You cannot assume that total sales in December are the same as in July, so you cannot answer this question. The answer is **(E)**.

Strategy Tip: Be careful of the difference between charts that show percentages and charts that show actual quantities.

Line Charts

Line charts are very similar to column charts, but each amount is shown as a floating dot instead of as a column, and the dots are connected by lines. As is true with column charts, often, the *x*-axis is time (e.g., months, years), and line charts are used to show trends over time. Because of the continuous nature of lines, data series that are shown in line charts are almost always continuous values for something, and not separate categories, as they sometimes are in column charts.

Here is an example showing the produce stand's sales in a line chart:

Some common calculations that you might be asked to perform are percentage increase or decrease from one time period to the next, the change in the overall average value of the data points if one of them changes, or even more simply, a count of the number of periods when data values were above or below a particular level:

Approximate percentage increase in sales from April to May:

$$\frac{\text{May sales} - \text{April sales}}{\text{April sales}} \approx \frac{5{,}021 - 4{,}441}{4{,}441} \approx 11\%$$

Number of months when sales were less than July sales is 11.

1. If the average sales per month at Produce Stand P were calculated at $4,725, and then it was discovered that the sales in January were actually $4,072 instead of the amount shown, what would the approximate correct average sales per month be?

   (A) $4,740   (B) $4,762   (C) $4,769   (D) $4,775   (E) Cannot be determined

The average sales per month is just the total of all the monthly sales divided by the number of months.

The only chart you have is this line chart, and it shows the monthly sales. The old amount for January was $3,890.

The average formula is:

$$\text{old average} = 4{,}725 = \frac{\text{sum of 12 months of sales}}{12}$$

$$\text{new average} = \frac{\text{sum of 12 months of sales} - 3{,}890 + 4{,}072}{12}$$

Since the total sum of the monthly sales has increased by 182, the average of the 12 monthly sales has increased by about $182 \div 12$ or about 15, so the answer is **(A)**.

You can verify that this is correct by examining the algebra:

$$\text{new average} = \frac{\text{sum of 12 months of sales} - 3{,}890 + 4{,}072}{12}$$

$$= \frac{\text{sum of 12 months of sales} + 182}{12}$$

$$= \frac{\text{sum of 12 months of sales}}{12} + \frac{182}{12}$$

$$\approx 4{,}725 + 15$$

$$= 4{,}740$$

The correct answer is **(A)**.

Problem Recap: The GRE likes these changing average problems. Remember the average change estimation shortcut!

2. What was the approximate percent increase in total sales at Produce Stand P from January to June?

   (A) 19%   (B) 24%   (C) 28%   (D) 32%   (E) 38%

In order to calculate the percent increase from January to June, you need the total sales in January and the total sales in June.

The only chart you have is this line chart, and it shows the monthly sales. The amount for January is $3,890 and the amount for June is $5,143.

The percent increase formula is:

$$\frac{\text{new} - \text{old}}{\text{old}} = \frac{\text{Jun sales} - \text{Jan sales}}{\text{Jan sales}}$$

$$\frac{\text{Jun sales} - \text{Jan sales}}{\text{Jan sales}} = \frac{5{,}143 - 3{,}890}{3{,}890} \approx 0.32$$

The answer is **(D)**.

Strategy Tip: Know the percent increase and decrease formulas!

Multi-Line Charts

The GRE is especially fond of multi-line charts because they can be used to show two or more data series at a time. Note that multi-line charts, like stacked and clustered column charts, have legends.

In the example below, you have vegetable sales and fruit sales. With line charts, you have to sum data points to calculate a total, because a total line is seldom shown (column charts are used when the goal is to emphasize the total).

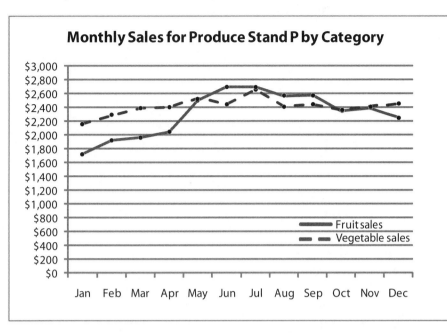

In addition to questions that require you to pick out data points from one of the data lines, expect that on at least a few questions you will be asked to either combine or compare the data that make up one line to the data that make up the other:

Approximate percentage increase in fruit sales from Jan to May:

$$\frac{\text{May sales} - \text{Jan sales}}{\text{Jan sales}} \approx \frac{2,500 - 1,700}{1,700} \approx 47\%$$

Number of months when vegetable sales were more than $100 greater than fruit sales is 6.

3. Over which of the following sequences of months did total sales decline the most?

   (A) Feb–Mar   (B) Mar–Apr   (C) Jun–Jul   (D) Aug–Sep   (E) Sep–Oct

Total sales are the sum of fruit and vegetable sales, and a decline means that at least one of the two would have to go down, and that drop would have to be bigger than any increase in the other category.

The only chart you have is this line chart, and it shows the monthly sales, although it doesn't add them up for you.

You hardly need a formula, because total sales are just the sum of fruit sales plus vegetable sales.

By scanning through the graph, you see that from Feb–Mar and Mar–Apr, both fruit and vegetable sales increased, so there was no decline. From Jun–Jul, vegetable sales increased, but fruit sales stayed flat, so still no decline. Aug–Sep also looks like a slight increase for both fruit and vegetable sales. However, from Sep–Oct, both fruit and vegetable sales seem to have declined, so the correct answer must be **(E)**.

The long way to do this problem is to read both fruit and vegetable sales and calculate approximate total sales for each month:

Feb sales = 1,900 + 2,300 = 4,200
Mar sales = 2,000 + 2,400 = 4,400   Increase of 200
Apr sales = 2,200 + 2,400 = 4,600   Increase of 200

Jun sales = 2,400 + 2,700 = 5,100   Increase of 300
Jul sales = 2,700 + 2,700 = 5,400

Aug sales = 2,400 + 2,600 = 5,000   No change
Sep sales = 2,400 + 2,600 = 5,000   At last! A monthly decrease
Oct sales = 2,400 + 2,400 = 4,800

This would take entirely too long!

Strategy Tip: Try visual estimation before performing calculations.

---

4. If the average price that the Produce Stand P sold fruit for in May was 80 cents per pound and the average wholesale cost to the Produce Stand in May for a pound of fruit was 25 cents per pound, approximately how much was produce stand P's gross profit on the sale of fruit in May?

   (A) $1,600   (B) $1,630   (C) $1,680   (D) $1,720   (E) Cannot be determined

To solve this, you need to remember that Gross profit = Sales revenue – Costs. If you can plug in for fruit sales revenue and fruit cost, you can answer this question.

The only chart you have is this line chart, and it shows the monthly fruit sales revenue in May, so you may be able to figure this out.

The answer choices are too close together to estimate, so you'll have to calculate.

You know that May fruit sales revenue is about $2,500. You know that the average wholesale cost per pound of fruit was $0.25 and that the average retail price per pound of fruit was $0.80. Thus:

Average gross profit per pound of fruit sold in May = 0.80 – 0.25 = 0.55

Gross profit on fruit sold in May = profit per pound × number of pounds of fruit sold
= 0.55 × number of pounds of fruit sold

$$\text{number of lbs of fruit sold in May} = \frac{\text{total fruit revenue}}{\text{revenue per lb}}$$

$$= \frac{2,500}{0.800} = 3,125$$

Gross profit on fruit sold in May = Profit per lb × Number of lbs of fruit sold
$$= 0.55 \times 3,125 = \$1,718.75$$

The answer is (**D**).

Strategy Tip: If you need a quantity, such as number of pounds of fruit sold, that is not directly shown in a graph, try writing out equations for it in terms of quantities you do know.

Bar Charts

A bar chart is essentially a column chart on its side. Although almost all bar charts on the GRE show absolute quantities, it is possible for them to show percentages. Because these more exotic charts are so rare on the GRE and are essentially types of column charts on their sides, this section focuses on standard bar charts.

The GRE generally represents a single data series in each bar chart, and, like pie charts, some bar charts include a total amount annotated on the chart.

Here is an example showing the April sales breakout by item for Produce Stand P. The length of each bar represents either an absolute number or a percentage. In this case, it's an absolute number:

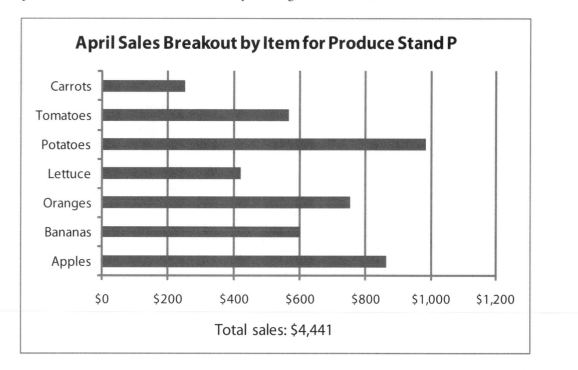

1. What fruit or vegetable generated the third highest sales in April for Produce Stand P?

    (A) tomatoes   (B) lettuce   (C) oranges   (D) bananas   (E) apples

The question asks you to figure out the fruit or vegetable that generated the third highest sales in the month of April.

The only chart you have is this bar chart, and it shows the sales for each fruit and vegetable in April.

Scanning the chart, you see that potatoes had the highest sales, then apples, and third were oranges. So the answer must be **(C)**.

Strategy Tip: Use a finger or a piece of paper to create a vertical line to help read bar chart values.

---

2. Which of the following ratios is closest to the ratio of carrot sales to potato sales at Produce Stand P in the month of April?

    (A) 1 : 4   (B) 2 : 9   (C) 1 : 5   (D) 1 : 6   (E) 3 : 10

In order to calculate the ratio of carrot sales to potato sales in April, you need to know those amounts, and the chart gives them to you.

The chart shows carrot sales were about \$250 and potato sales were about \$980:

$$\frac{\text{carrot sales}}{\text{potato sales}} = \frac{250}{980} \approx 0.255 \approx \frac{1}{4}$$

The answer is **(A)**.

Tables

A table is a very straightforward way to present data when calculations using that data are required because there is no need to estimate numbers. The thing that a table doesn't do, though, is allow you to easily see trends or estimate using visual techniques.

Often, one table will contain a mix of absolute quantities and percentage data. Be careful not to confuse the two. The GRE does not always label individual percents with a percentage sign. Rather, the entire row or column is generally labeled as such in the row or column header.

8

If you have to do calculations, and you probably will if you are given a table, it will be easy to look up the numbers. Here is an example of a table that combines absolute quantity information with percentage information for the produce stand:

Monthly Sales Breakout for Produce Stand P

Month	Total (in Dollars)	% Fruit	% Vegetable
Jan	4,121	44.29	55.71
Feb	4,204	45.74	54.26
Mar	4,361	45.10	54.90
Apr	4,568	49.99	54.06
May	4,791	49.17	50.83
Jun	4,756	52.40	47.60
Jul	4,822	50.38	49.62
Aug	4,791	51.41	48.59
Sep	4,801	51.21	48.79
Oct	4,726	49.89	50.11
Nov	4,817	49.78	50.22
Dec	4,881	47.77	52.23

1. Approximately how many dollars' worth of vegetables were sold in September, October, and November combined by Produce Stand P?

(A) $5,724   (B) $6,230   (C) $6,621   (D) $7,130   (E) $7,685

The question asks you to calculate the dollars' worth of vegetable sales in September, October, and November.

You can do this because the chart shows the total sales for each month and the percentage of those sales that were due to vegetables. In September, vegetable sales were 48.79% of $4,801; in October, 50.11% of $4,726; and in November, 50.22% of $4,817. Next, calculate as follows:

$$\text{Sep + Oct + Nov vegetable sales} = (0.4879 \times 4{,}801) + (0.5011 \times 4{,}726) + (0.5022 \times 4{,}817)$$
$$= 2{,}342.41 + 2{,}368.20 + 2.419.10$$
$$= 7{,}129.71$$

The answer is (**D**).

8

Other Common Types of Diagrams

Occasionally, other common types of diagrams, such as floor plans or outline maps, appear on the GRE. The good news is that although these diagrams are a little less familiar than the basic five, the questions that go with them tend to be a little bit easier. There are questions that ask you to calculate surface area (of walls) and volume of rooms, but far fewer of the more challenging percent change and "how many points satisfy this complicated set of criteria" variety.

Questions That Typically Require Input from More Than One Graph to Solve

So far, you've looked at the usual types of charts seen in GRE Data Interpretation and typical questions based on those charts. However, the GRE often complicates things by asking questions that require that you look up and integrate information from multiple charts. This type of multi-chart question is not mathematically harder than a single-graph question, but since it requires using data from two different graphs, it can be a bit more confusing. Efficient solving techniques and good scrap paper organization become even more valuable with multiple charts, because more charts mean more opportunities to become confused and waste time. The next example combines two types of charts that you've seen before, and asks questions that require using information from both of them:

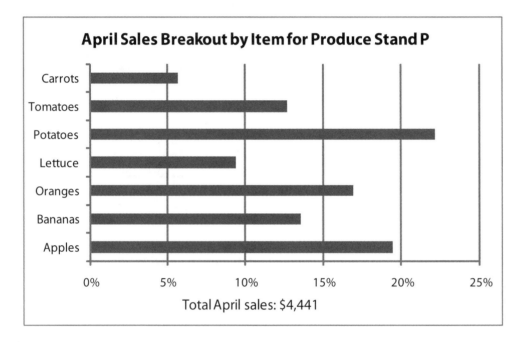

Vitamin Content of Produce Items Sold at Produce Stand P in April

	Vitamin C Content	**Vitamin A Content**
Apples	low	low
Bananas	medium	low
Oranges	high	medium
Lettuce	high	low
Potatoes	medium	low
Tomatoes	high	high
Carrots	low	high

1. Approximately what were the total April sales of produce items at Produce Stand P that were high in both vitamin A and vitamin C content?

   (A) 451   (B) 488   (C) 577   (D) 624   (E) 683

You need to figure out which produce items were high in both vitamin A and vitamin C and calculate the total sales of those items.

The table shows you that only tomatoes are high in both vitamins A and C, so you need total tomato sales.

The bar graph shows you that tomatoes account for about 13% of April sales and that total April sales were $4,441. So you need 13% of $4,441:

$$0.13 \times 4,441 = \$577.33$$

The answer is **(C)**.

2. Approximately what dollar amount of the produce sold by Produce Stand P in April had medium or high amounts of either vitamin A or vitamin C?

   (A) $3,120   (B) $3,600   (C) $4,000   (D) $4,600   (E) Cannot be determined

You need to figure out which produce items were high or medium in either vitamin A or vitamin C and calculate the total sales of those items.

The table shows you that bananas, oranges, lettuce, potatoes, tomatoes, and carrots are high in either vitamin A or vitamin C, so you need their total sales.

Since most of the produce items are high or medium in either vitamin A or vitamin C, it will be faster to just calculate the dollar amount of the items sold that are low in both vitamin A and vitamin C and subtract that from the total dollar amount of sales. The table shows that the only produce item that meets these criteria is apples, and the bar graph shows that they accounted for about 19% of total sales:

$$0.19 \times 4,441 \approx 844$$

$$4,441 - 844 = 3,597$$

The answer is **(B)**.

8

The long way to do this problem is to sum up the percentages of each type of produce that has a medium or high level of vitamin A or vitamin C.

To do this, you need to read a number of values off of the bar graph. Carrots are ≈ 6% of sales, tomatoes are ≈ 13%, potatoes are ≈ 22%, lettuce is ≈ 9%, oranges are ≈ 17%, and bananas are ≈ 14%. Thus:

$$(0.06 \times 4{,}441) + (0.13 \times 4{,}441) + (0.22 \times 4{,}441) + (0.17 \times 4{,}441) + (0.14 \times 4{,}441)$$
$$= (0.06 + 0.13 + 0.22 + 0.09 + 0.17 + 0.14) \times 4{,}441$$
$$= 0.81 \times 4{,}441$$
$$= 3{,}597$$

That was too much work!

Strategy Tip: Sometimes it is easier to calculate the percentage that does *not* satisfy a condition rather than calculate a percentage directly.

8

This page left intentionally blank.

A Straightforward Data Interpretation Problem Set

Here is some practice on a straightforward Data Interpretation problem. Start by reading the question and the answers, and formulating your plan of attack.

Problem A

The preceding three graphs are the data for the five questions that follow. Since you've read this chapter, you know that it is a good idea to scan the graphs before looking at the problems to get a general sense of what information the graphs contain.

1. In how many years shown was the average duration of visits to Aquarium A more than twice as much as the average in 1985?

   (A) Four   (B) Three   (C) Two   (D) One   (E) None

2. In 1980, if a full-price ticket cost $4.70, what would have been the average daily revenue, in thousands of dollars, from the sale of full-price tickets?

   ☐

3. In 2000, the total number of dollars of gift shop revenue was how many times as great as the average daily number of full-price tickets sold?

   (A) 400   (B) 200   (C) 80   (D) 40   (E) 20

4. What was the approximate percent increase in average daily full-price ticket sales from 1990 to 1995?

   (A) 10%   (B) 20%   (C) 33%   (D) 48%   (E) 66%

5. Which of the following statements can be inferred from the data?

   ☐ In each of the 5-year periods shown in which yearly gift shop revenue decreased, average daily full-price ticket sales also decreased.

   ☐ The greatest increase in total yearly gift shop revenue over any 5-year period shown was $2.7 million.

   ☐ From 1995 to 2000, the average duration of visits to the museum increased by 12 minutes.

An Example Mixing Percents and Absolute Quantities

It is very common in GRE Data Interpretation problems to see a set of graphs that incorporate both percentage and absolute quantity data. Being able to quickly and confidently combine these two types of data is a critical success factor for many medium to hard DI problems. The following problems are typical examples:

Problem B

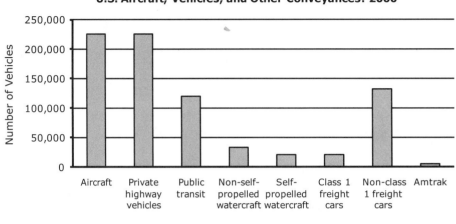

U.S. Aircraft, Vehicles, and Other Conveyances: 2000

Total conveyances: 785,000

Private Highway Vehicles: 2000

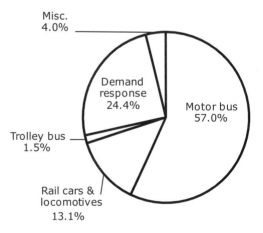

Public Transit Vehicles: 2000

If you scanned the graphs before looking at the problems, you know that the graphs have to do with absolute numbers of vehicles (the bar graph) and some additional information on the percentages of specific types of public transit and private highway vehicles in 2000. Also notice that the bar graph has a total conveyances line at the bottom, which may prove useful.

1. Approximately what was the ratio of trucks to passenger cars?

   (A) 1 to 20   (B) 1 to 18   (C) 1 to 17   (D) 1 to 15   (E) 1 to 12

2. Approximately how many more miscellaneous public transit vehicles than public transit trolley buses were there in 2000?

   (A) 1,000   (B) 1,500   (C) 2,000   (D) 2,500   (E) 3,000

3. If the number of aircraft, vehicles, and other conveyances was 572,000 in 1995, what was the approximate percentage increase from 1995 to 2000?

   (A) 37%   (B) 32%   (C) 27%   (D) 20%   (E) 15%

4. In 2000, if an equal percentage of passenger cars and demand-response vehicles experienced mechanical problems, and the number of passenger cars that experienced such problems was 13,436, approximately how many demand-response vehicles experienced mechanical problems?

   (A) 1,352   (B) 2,928   (C) 4,099   (D) 7,263   (E) 9,221

8

A Very Challenging Example, Requiring Excellent Technique

The following set is tricky. The graphs are a bit more complicated than is typical on the GRE. (Note that, because the GRE is a section-level adaptive test, only those who performed at a high level on their first Quant section would ever see a Data Interpretation set this difficult.)

Problem C

Natural Resource Industries' Output as a Percentage of Gross Domestic Product in Province P

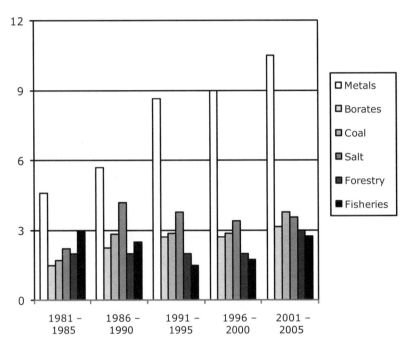

Mining Industries' Average Annual Production

| Years | Mining Industries' Average Annual Production, in millions of 2005 dollars | Percentage of Mining Industries' Production | | | | | |
| | | Metals | | | Other Mined Products | | |
		Uranium, Titanium, & Aluminum	Gold & Silver	Copper	Borates	Coal	Salt
1981–1985	$342.5	10%	20%	16%	15%	17%	22%
1986–1990	$326.8	12	17	9	15	19	28
1991–1995	$310.0	16	20	12	15	16	21
1996–2000	$257.9	12	22	16	15	16	19
2001–2005	$205.0	14	24	12	15	18	17

1. Approximately what percent of the mining industries' average annual production from 1991–1995 came from production of aluminum?

   (A) 4%   (B) 7%   (C) 11%   (D) 22%   (E) Cannot be determined

2. Approximately what percent of average annual GDP of Province P from 1996–2000 came from copper production?

   (A) 3%   (B) 6%   (C) 9%   (D) 14%   (E) 18%

3. Which of the following statements can be inferred from the information given?

   ☐ For all the time periods shown, borate production, in millions of 2005 dollars, was the same.

   ☐ Of the time periods shown, 1981–1985 was the one in which the mining industries produced the greatest value of gold and silver, measured in 2005 dollars.

   ☐ Of the time periods shown, 2001–2005 had the highest average annual GDP, measured in 2005 dollars.

8

Problem Set Solutions

Problem A

1. **(C):** First, identify the chart that gives information about the average duration of visits: the bottom graph. The question asks for the number of years shown that had an average duration of more than twice the average in 1985.

The average duration in 1985 was 45 minutes, so find the number of years that had an average duration greater than 90 minutes. Only 1995 and 2000 fit this constraint, so the answer is two, choice (C).

2. **235:** The average daily revenue for the aquarium can be found using the following formula:

$$\text{avg. daily revenue} = \left(\frac{\$}{\text{ticket}}\right) \times \text{avg. \# of tickets}$$

The price per ticket is given in the question ($4.70), and the top graph gives the average daily number of tickets sold. In 1980, the average daily number of tickets sold was 50,000, so the average daily revenue is 50,000 × $4.70 = $235,000. The question asks for the revenue in thousands, so the answer is 235.

3. **(D):** To answer this question, you'll need information about both gift shop revenue and the average number of full-price tickets sold. The former can be found in the middle graph, and the latter can be found in the top graph.

In 2000, total gift shop revenue for the year was $3,600,000 and the average daily number of full-price tickets sold was 90,000. The question asks how many times greater 3,600,000 is than 90,000. To find out, divide 3,600,000 by 90,000 (using the calculator!).

The answer is 40, choice (D).

4. **(D):** Percent increase is defined as the change divided by the original value. In this question then, the percent increase can be found using the following formula (let x stand for the average daily full-price ticket sales):

$$\frac{(x \text{ in } 1995) - (x \text{ in } 1990)}{(x \text{ in } 1990)}$$

Information on the average number of full-price ticket sales can be found in the top graph. The average number in 1990 was 220 and in 1995 it was 325:

$$\frac{325 - 220}{220} = \frac{105}{220} = 0.477$$

Remember that the question asks you to approximate. The answer is closest to choice (D).

5. **Statement II only**. Since this question asks which statements can be inferred from the data, you have to use the process of elimination and treat each statement as its own mini question.

First statement: Identify the 5-year periods in which gift shop revenue (middle graph) decreased: 1990–1995 & 1995–2000. Next, locate the graph for average ticket sales, which is the top graph. Ticket sales did *not* decrease in 1990–1995, so statement I is false.

Second statement: The graph for gift shop revenue is the middle one. Locate the biggest jump—it is from 2.3 to 5. Compute the size of this jump: $5 - 2.3 = 2.7$, so statement II is true.

Third statement: The graph for duration of visits is the bottom one. The increase from 1995–2000 was $104 - 97$, which equals 7 minutes, not 12 minutes, so statement III is false.

Only the box for the second statement should be selected.

Problem B

1. **(D):** For specific information about trucks and passenger cars, look at the middle graph. Though the pie chart does not give specific information about the number of cars or the number of trucks, it does tell you what percent of the total number of private vehicles each represents. Because each of the percents is out of the same total, you can compare the percents directly to find the ratio of cars to trucks.

Note: You could also use the information in the top graph to calculate the actual numbers of cars and trucks, but that would be time-consuming and unnecessary.

Remember that the question asks you to approximate. The ratio of 4% to 59.5% is approximately the ratio of 4 to 60. Reduce the ratio to get the correct answer, 1 : 15.

2. **(E):** To find the total numbers of miscellaneous public transit vehicles and public transit trolley buses, you will need to combine information from the top and bottom graphs.

According to the top graph, there were roughly 120,000 public transit vehicles in 2000 (remember the question asks you to approximate). Of those 120,000 public transit vehicles, 4% were miscellaneous vehicles and 1.5% were trolley buses.

The difference in the number of miscellaneous and trolley bus vehicles is:

$$(0.04 \times 120{,}000) - (0.015 \times 120{,}000)$$

Either calculate both numbers and subtract, or realize that the difference will be $(0.04 - 0.015) \times 120{,}000$. However you perform the calculation, the difference is 3,000.

3. **(A):** Percent increase is defined as change divided by original value. In this question then, the percent increase can be found using the following formula (let x stand for the total number of U.S. aircraft, vehicles, and other conveyances):

$$\frac{(x \text{ in } 2000) - (x \text{ in } 1995)}{(x \text{ in } 1995)}$$

The question says that the total number in 1995 was 572,000. The total number in 2000 can be found in the top graph. Fortunately, the question doesn't require you to add the values in every column together! At the bottom, the graph states that the total number of conveyances was 785,000.

Find the approximate percent increase:

$$\frac{785,000 - 572,000}{572,000} = 0.372 \approx 37\%$$

Answer choice (A) is the closest to the real value.

4. **(B):** Rephrase the question as a mathematical expression. To save time, write x for "the number of demand-response vehicles that experience mechanical problems" when you rephrase the question. The key thing to remember here is the relationship between percentages and absolute numbers. Multiply the percentage times the total to get the absolute quantity:

$$\text{If } \frac{13,436}{\text{total number passenger cars}} = \frac{x}{\text{total number dem-resp vehicles}} \text{ , then what is } x?$$

$$\text{Rearrange to get: } x = \frac{13,436 \times (\text{total number dem-resp vehicles})}{\text{total number passenger cars}}$$

You know from the first pie that demand-response vehicles makes up 24.4% of all public transit vehicles, and you know from the main chart that there are roughly 120,000 public transit vehicles, so you can calculate the approximate number of demand-response vehicles:

$$0.244 \times 120,000 = 29,280$$

You know from the second pie that passenger cars makes up 59.5% of all private highway vehicles, and you know from the main chart that there are about 225,000 private highway vehicles, so you can calculate the approximate number of private highway vehicles:

$$0.595 \times 225,000 = 133,875$$

8

So, pulling it all together:

$$x = \frac{13,436 \times 29,280}{133,875} \approx 2,938$$

To avoid overloading the calculator display, you must divide 13,436 by 133,875 before multiplying by 29,280.

The answer is (B).

Problem C

1. **(E):** Since one of the answer choices is "cannot be determined," check exact wording and be sure you have enough information to solve it before doing any math.

Locate the relevant column within the table in the chart on the bottom: "Uranium, Titanium, & Aluminum." The figures in this column represent Uranium + Titanium + Aluminum, but do not tell you the level of Aluminum *alone*. Since the question is asking *only* about Aluminum, you do not have enough information.

The answer is (E).

Strategy Tip: This type of problem is very quick if you check to see whether you have enough information to answer the question before making any calculations.

---

2. **(A):**Rephrase the question. Expressing the desired percentage as a fraction is a good way to abbreviate the question:

$$\text{In } 1996 - 2000, \frac{\text{Copper}}{\text{GDP}} = ?$$

The chart that mentions Copper is on the bottom and tells you that from 1996–2000, Copper was 16% of Mining Industries' Production. In other words, it tells you that the value of $\frac{\text{Copper}}{\text{Mining}} = 0.16$. This is not quite what you are looking for, since the question is about $\frac{\text{Copper}}{\text{GDP}}$. Look to the top chart to see if it provides a way to convert your $\frac{\text{Copper}}{\text{Mining}}$ information into a $\frac{\text{Copper}}{\text{GDP}}$ figure.

The top chart gives you information on Metals, Borates, Coal, and Salt—all of the components of Mining from the bottom table—as a percentage of GDP. You will therefore be able to use the following equation to get $\frac{\text{Copper}}{\text{GDP}}$:

$$\frac{\text{Copper}}{\text{GDP}} = \left(\frac{\text{Copper}}{\text{Mining}} \right) \times \left(\frac{\text{Mining}}{\text{GDP}} \right)$$

Substitute numbers into the above equation. The top chart tells you that from 1996–2000, Metals were 9% of GDP and Borates, Coal, and Salt were each roughly 3% of GDP. Thus, total Mining was roughly 9% + 3% + 3% + 3%, or 18% of GDP.

$$\frac{\text{Copper}}{\text{GDP}} = \left(\frac{\text{Copper}}{\text{Mining}} \right) \times \left(\frac{\text{Mining}}{\text{GDP}} \right)$$

$$\approx (16\%) \times (18\%) = (0.16) \times (0.18) = 0.029 \approx 3\%$$

The answer is (A).

Strategy Tip: Write out equations with units to help yourself figure out what values you need.

---

3. **Statement II only.** First statement: For each time period, the production of Borates, in the bottom chart, is given as 15% of that period's Mining Industries' Production. Since each period has a *different* dollar figure for Mining Industries' Production, Borate production is not the same in all of the periods. (For example, from 1981–1985, Borate production was 15% × $342.5, whereas from 1986–1990, Borate production was 15% × $326.8.) Statement I is therefore false.

Second statement: To test whether this is true, notice that the dollar values of Gold & Silver production were:

    81–85: 20% × $342.5
    86–90: 17% × $326.8
    91–95: 20% × $310
    96–00: 22% × $257.9
    01–05: 24% × $205

You can eliminate two of these five choices without doing any arithmetic. The figure for 86–90 is clearly lower than that for 81–85, because 86–90 has a lower percentage (17% as opposed to 20%) times a lower dollar amount ($326.8 as opposed to $342.5). Along the same lines, you can see that 91–95 is lower than 81–85: the percentage is the same for both periods (20%), but for 91–95 that percentage is multiplied by a smaller dollar amount ($310 as opposed to $342.5). For the three remaining periods, use the calculator:

    81–85: 20% × $342.5 = 68.50
    96–00: 22% × $257.9 = 56.74
    01–05: 24% × $205 = 49.20

These calculations show that 81–85 had the highest Gold & Silver production, so statement II is true.

Third statement: It concerns which period had the highest Gross Domestic Product (GDP). You clearly need to use the TOP chart, because it is the one that mentions GDP. However, the top chart is not enough, because it only gives information as *percentages*. To get dollar amounts for GDP, you need to connect the dollar amounts in the *bottom* chart with the percentages in the top chart.

One way to figure out GDP in 2001–2005 would be to focus on Salt. The top table gives a figure for Salt as a percentage of GDP (roughly 3.5%), and the bottom table allows you to figure out the dollar amount of Salt production (17% × $205). Substituting these figures into the following equation, you could solve for GDP:

$$GDP = \frac{Salt}{\left(\dfrac{Salt}{GDP}\right)}$$

$$GDP = \frac{0.17 \times \$205}{3.596}$$

However, performing this calculation, and similar calculations for other time periods, would be too much work. It is a good idea to focus on Borates instead, since Borates accounted for the *same* percentage (15%) of Mining Industries' Production in each of the time periods shown. Consider the equation:

$$GDP = \frac{Borates}{\left(\dfrac{Borates}{GDP}\right)}$$

Compare 1981–1985 to 2001–2005. In 2001–2005, the numerator (Borates) of the fraction $\dfrac{Borates}{\left(\dfrac{Borates}{GDP}\right)}$ was *lower* than in any other time period—it was 15% of the *lowest* value ($205 million) for Mining Industries' Production. On the other hand, 2001–2005 saw the denominator $\left(\dfrac{Borates}{GDP}\right)$ of our large fraction assume its *highest* value (≈ 3%), because the top chart shows that 2001–2005 was the only time frame in which Borate production was more than 3% of GDP. Thus, $GDP = \dfrac{(0.015) \times (205 \text{ million})}{0.03}$ for 2001–2005.

From 1981–1985, Borates were 15% of a much greater total ($342.5 million), but were a smaller percentage of GDP (≈ 1.5%). So $GDP = \dfrac{(0.015) \times (342.5 \text{ million})}{0.015}$. This fraction has a larger numerator and a smaller denominator, which will result in a higher total GDP. Statement III is therefore false.

Only the box for the second statement should be checked.

Strategy Tip: On problems this difficult, it is essential to **avoid hard math** even with a calculator, and rely on approximation and bounding instead. Using the calculator is helpful, but always look for quicker ways to arrive at a conclusion.

MANHATTAN
PREP

Appendix A
of

Quantitative Comparisons
& Data Interpretation

GRE Math Glossary

absolute value: The distance from zero on the number line for a particular term (e.g., the absolute value of −7 is 7—written |−7|).

arc length: A section of a circle's circumference.

area: The space enclosed by a given closed shape on a plane; the formula depends on the specific shape (e.g., the area of a rectangle equals *length × width*).

axis: One of the two number lines (*x*-axis or *y*-axis) used to indicate position on a coordinate plane. (See figure)

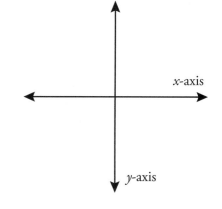

base: In the expression b^n, the variable *b* represents the base. This is the number that you multiply by itself *n* times. Also can refer to the horizontal side of a triangle.

center (circle): The point from which any point on a circle's radius is equidistant.

central angle: The angle created by any two radii. (See figure)

circle: A set of points in a plane that are equidistant from a fixed center point.

circumference: The measure of the perimeter of a circle. The circumference of a circle can be found with this formula: $C = 2\pi r$, where *C* is the circumference and *r* is the radius.

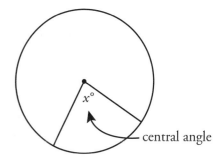

coefficient: A number being multiplied by a variable. In the equation $y = 2x + 5$, the coefficient of the *x* term is 2.

common denominator: When adding or subtracting fractions, you first must find a common denominator, generally the smallest common multiple of both numbers.

Example:

>   Given (3/5) + (1/2), the two denominators are 5 and 2. The smallest multiple that works for both numbers is 10. The common denominator, therefore, is 10.

composite number: Any number that has more than two factors. Thus, composite numbers are not prime.

constant: A number that doesn't change, in an equation or expression. You may not know its value, but it's "constant" in contrast to a variable, which varies. In the equation $y = 3x + 2$, 3 and 2 are constants. In the equation of a line, $y = mx + b$, m and b are constants, even if you do not necessarily know their values.

coordinate plane: Consists of a horizontal axis (typically labeled "*x*") and a vertical axis (typically labeled "*y*"), crossing at the number zero on both axes.

decimal: Numbers that fall in between integers. A decimal can express a part-to-whole relationship, just as a percent or fraction can.

Example:

> The number 1.2 is a decimal. The integers 1 and 2 are not decimals. An integer written as 1.0, however, is considered a decimal. The decimal 0.2 is equivalent to 20% or to 2/10 (= 1/5).

denominator: The bottom of a fraction. In the fraction (7/2), 2 is the denominator.

diameter: A line segment that passes through the center of a circle and whose endpoints lie on the circle.

difference: When one number is subtracted from another, the difference is what is left over. The difference of 7 and 5 is 2, because $7 - 5 = 2$.

digit: The ten numbers 0, 1, 2, 3, 4, 5, 6, 7, 8, and 9. Used in combination to represent other numbers (e.g., 12 or 0.38).

distributed form: Presenting an expression as a sum or difference. In distributed form, terms are added or subtracted. For example, $x^2 - 1$ is in distributed form, as is $x^2 + 2x + 1$. In contrast, $(x + 1)(x - 1)$ is not in distributed form; it is in factored form.

divisible: If an integer x divided by another number y yields an integer, then x is said to be divisible by y.

Example:

> The number 12 divided by 3 yields the integer 4. Therefore, 12 is divisible by 3. However, 12 divided by 5 does not yield an integer. Therefore, 12 is not divisible by 5.

divisor: The part of a division operation that comes after the division sign. In the operation $22 \div 4$ (or 22/4), 4 is the divisor. Divisor is also a synonym for factor. (See *factor*)

equation: A combination of mathematical expressions and symbols that contains an equals sign. For example, $3 + 7 = 10$ is an equation, as is $x + y = 3$. An equation makes a statement: left side equals right side.

equilateral triangle: A triangle in which all three angles are equal (and since the three angles in a triangle always add to 180°, each angle is equal to 60°). In addition, all three sides are of equal length.

even: An integer is even if it is divisible by 2. For example, 14 is even because 14/2 equals the integer 7.

exponent: In the expression b^n, the variable n represents the exponent. The exponent indicates how many times to multiply the base, b, by itself. For example, $4^3 = 4 \times 4 \times 4$, or 4 multiplied by itself three times.

expression: A combination of numbers and mathematical symbols that does not contain an equals sign. For example, xy is an expression, as is $x + 3$. An expression represents a quantity.

factor: Positive integers that divide evenly into an integer. Factors are equal to or smaller than the integer in question. For example, 12 is a factor of 12, as are 1, 2, 3, 4, and 6.

factored form: Presenting an expression as a product. In factored form, expressions are multiplied together. The expression $(x + 1)(x - 1)$ is in factored form: $(x + 1)$ and $(x - 1)$ are the factors. In contrast, $x^2 - 1$ is not in factored form; it is in distributed form.

factor foundation rule: If a is a factor of b, and b is a factor of c, then a is also a factor of c. For example, 2 is a factor of 10 and 10 is a factor of 60. Therefore, 2 is also a factor of 60.

factor tree: Use the "factor tree" to break any number down into its prime factors. For example: →

FOIL: First, Outside, Inside, Last; an acronym to remember the method for converting from factored to distributed form in a quadratic equation or expression. For example, $(x + 2)(x - 3)$ is a quadratic expression in factored form. Multiply the First, Outside, Inside, and Last terms to get the distributed form: $x \times x = x^2$, $x \times -3 = -3x$, $x \times 2 = 2x$, and $2 \times -3 = -6$. The full distributed form is $x^2 - 3x + 2x - 6$. This can be simplified to $x^2 - x - 6$.

fraction: A way to express numbers that fall in between integers (though integers can also be expressed in fractional form). A fraction expresses a part-to-whole relationship in terms of a numerator (the part) and a denominator (the whole); for example, 3/4 is a fraction.

hypotenuse: The longest side of a right triangle. The hypotenuse is always the side opposite the largest angle of a triangle, so in a right triangle, it is opposite the right angle.

improper fraction: Fractions that are greater than 1. An improper can also be written as a mixed number. For example, 7/2 is an improper fraction. This can also be written as a mixed number: $3\dfrac{1}{2}$.

inequality: A comparison of quantities that have different values. There are four ways to express inequalities: less than (<), less than or equal to (≤), greater than (>), or greater than or equal to (≥). Can be manipulated in the same way as equations with one exception: when multiplying or dividing by a negative number, the inequality sign flips.

integers: Numbers, such as −1, 0, 1, 2, and 3, that have no fractional part. Integers include the counting numbers (1, 2, 3, …), their negative counterparts (−1, −2, −3, …), and 0.

interior angles: The angles that appear in the interior of a closed shape.

isosceles triangle: A triangle in which two of the three angles are equal; in addition, the sides opposite the two angles are equal in length.

line: A set of points that extend infinitely in one direction without curving. On the GRE, lines are by definition perfectly straight.

line segment: A continuous, finite section of a line. The sides of a triangle or of a rectangle are line segments.

linear equation: An equation that does not contain exponents or multiple variables multiplied together. For example, $x + y = 3$ is a linear equation; $xy = 3$ and $y = x^2$ are not. When plotted on a coordinate plane, linear equations create lines.

mixed number: An integer combined with a proper fraction. A mixed number can also be written as an improper fraction: $3\frac{1}{2}$ is a mixed number. This can also be written as an improper fraction, 7/2.

multiple: Multiples are integers formed by multiplying some integer by any other integer. For example, 12 is a multiple of 12 (12×1), as are 24 (= 12×2), 36 (= 12×3), 48 (= 12×4), and 60 (= 12×5). (Negative multiples are possible in mathematics but are not typically tested on the GRE.)

negative: Any number to the left of zero on a number line; can be an integer or non-integer.

negative exponent: Any exponent less than zero. To find a value for a term with a negative exponent, put the term containing the exponent in the denominator of a fraction and make the exponent positive: $4^{-2} = 1/4^2$; $1/3^{-2} = 1/(1/3)^2 = 3^2 = 9$.

number line: A picture of a straight line that represents all the numbers from negative infinity to infinity.

numerator: The top of a fraction. In the fraction, 7/2, 7 is the numerator.

odd: An integer that is not divisible by 2. For example, 15 is odd because 15/2 is not an integer (7.5).

order of operations: The order in which mathematical operations must be carried out in order to simplify an expression. (See *PEMDAS*)

the origin: The coordinate pair (0,0) represents the origin of a coordinate plane.

parallelogram: A four-sided, closed shape composed of straight lines in which the opposite sides are equal and the opposite angles are equal. (See figure)

PEMDAS: An acronym that stands for Parentheses, Exponents, Multiplication, Division, Addition, Subtraction; used to remember the order of operations.

percent: Literally, "per one hundred"; expresses a special part-to-whole relationship between a number (the part) and one hundred (the whole). A special type of fraction or decimal that involves the number 100 (e.g., 50% = 50 out of 100).

perimeter: In a polygon, the sum of the lengths of the sides.

perpendicular: Lines that intersect at a 90° angle.

plane: A flat, two-dimensional surface that extends infinitely in every direction.

point: An object that exists in a single location on the coordinate plane. Each point has a unique x-coordinate and y-coordinate that together describe its location (e.g., $(1, -2)$ is a point).

polygon: A two-dimensional, closed shape made of line segments. For example, a triangle is a polygon, as is a rectangle. A circle is a closed shape, but it is not a polygon because it does not contain line segments.

positive: Any number to the right of zero on a number line; can be an integer or non-integer.

prime factorization: A number expressed as a product of prime numbers. For example, the prime factorization of 60 is $2 \times 2 \times 3 \times 5$.

prime number: A positive integer with exactly two factors: 1 and itself. The number 1 does not qualify as prime because it has only one factor, not two. The number 2 is the smallest prime number; it is also the only even prime number. The numbers 2, 3, 5, 7, 11, 13, etc. are prime.

product: The end result when two numbers are multiplied together (e.g., the product of 4 and 5 is 20).

Pythagorean Theorem: A formula used to calculate the sides of a right triangle: $a^2 + b^2 = c^2$, where a and b are the lengths of the two legs of the triangle and c is the length of the hypotenuse of the triangle.

Pythagorean triplet: A set of three numbers that describes the lengths of the three sides of a right triangle in which all three sides have integer lengths. Common Pythagorean triplets are 3–4–5, 6–8–10, and 5–12–13.

quadrant: One quarter of the coordinate plane. Bounded on two sides by the x-axis and y-axis. Often labeled I, II, III, and IV. (See figure)

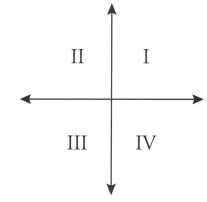

quadratic expression: An expression including a variable raised to the second power (and no higher powers). Commonly of the form $ax^2 + bx + c$, where a, b, and c are constants.

quotient: The result of dividing one number by another. The quotient of $10 \div 5$ is 2.

radius: A line segment that connects the center of a circle with any point on that circle's circumference. Plural: radii.

reciprocal: The product of a number and its reciprocal is always 1. To get the reciprocal of a number, divide 1 by that number. So the reciprocal of 2 is 1/2 and the reciprocal of (2/3) is 1/(2/3) = (3/2). This works even if the number is a decimal, so the reciprocal of 0.25 is 1/0.25 = 4.

rectangle: A four-sided closed shape in which all of the angles equal 90° and in which the opposite sides are equal. Rectangles are also parallelograms.

right triangle: A triangle that includes a 90°, or right, angle.

root: The opposite of an exponent (in a sense). The square root of 16 (written $\sqrt{16}$) is the number (or numbers) that, when multiplied by itself, will yield 16. In this case, both 4 and −4 would multiply to 16 mathematically. However, when the GRE provides the root sign for an even root, such as a square root, then the only accepted answer is the positive root, 4. That is, $\sqrt{16} = 4$, *not* +4 or −4. In contrast, the equation $x^2 = 16$ has *two* solutions, +4 and −4.

sector: A wedge of the circle, composed of two radii and the arc connecting those two radii. (See figure)

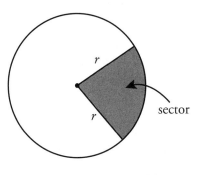

simplify: Reduce numerators and denominators to the smallest form by taking out common factors. Dividing the numerator and denominator by the same number does not change the value of the fraction.

Example:

> Given (21/6), you can simplify by dividing both the numerator and the denominator by 3. The simplified fraction is (7/2).

slope: Rise over run, or the distance the line runs vertically divided by the distance the line runs horizontally. The slope of any given line is constant over the length of that line. In the example shown, the slope of the line is 2, because from the leftmost labeled point to the rightmost labeled point, the line goes up 2 units and over 1 unit, and 2/1 = 2. (See figure)

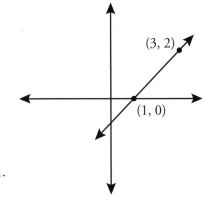

square: A four-sided, closed shape in which all of the angles equal 90° and all of the sides are equal. Squares are also rectangles and parallelograms.

sum: The result when two numbers are added together. The sum of 4 and 7 is 11.

term: Parts within an expression or equation that are separated by either a plus sign or a minus sign (e.g., in the expression $x + 3$, x and 3 are each separate terms).

triangle: A three-sided, closed shape composed of straight lines; the interior angles add up to 180°.

two-dimensional: A shape containing a length and a width.

variable: A letter used as a substitute for an unknown value, or number. Common letters for variables are x, y, z, and t. In contrast to a constant, you can generally think of a variable as a value that can change (hence the term variable). In the equation $y = 3x + 2$, both y and x are variables.

***x*-axis:** A horizontal number line that indicates left–right position on a coordinate plane.

x-coordinate: The number that indicates where a point lies along the *x*-axis. Always written first in parentheses. The *x*-coordinate of (2, −1) is 2.

x-intercept: The point where a line crosses the *x*-axis (that is, when $y = 0$). (See figure)

y-axis: A vertical number line that indicates up–down position on a coordinate plane.

y-coordinate: The number that indicates where a point lies along the *y*-axis. Always written second in parentheses. The *y*-coordinate of (2, −1) is −1.

y-intercept: The point where a line crosses the *y*-axis (that is, when $x = 0$). In the equation of a line $y = mx + b$, the *y*-intercept equals *b*. Technically, the coordinates of the *y*-intercept are (0, *b*). (See figure)

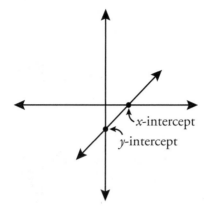

x-intercept
y-intercept

STUDY ANYWHERE!

WITH MANHATTAN PREP'S GRE FLASH CARDS

With our flashcards you can study both math and verbal concepts on the go!

Both our 500 Essential Words and a 500 Advanced Words cards go above and beyond providing abstract, out-of-context definitions. Complete with definitions, example sentences, pronunciations, and related words, this two-volume set comprises the most comprehensive vocabulary study tool on the market.

Our GRE Math Flash Cards provide practical exposure to the basic math concepts tested on the GRE.

Designed to be user-friendly for all students, these cards include easy-to-follow explanations of math concepts that promise to enhance comprehension and build fundamental skills.

NEED MORE THAN BOOKS ALONE?

TRY OUR GUIDED SELF-STUDY PROGRAM!

With over 27 hours of recorded video lessons, Guided Self-Study is a perfect fit for self-motivated individuals who want full access to all of Manhattan Prep's materials.

Armed with our syllabus and online resources suite, you can get more out of your books. This program is a great fit for students operating under a tight deadline or rigid schedule who may not have the time to take a live prep course.

Check it out at manhattanprep.com/gre/gre-self-study.cfm